# THE MISSION OF LOVE

## A SACRAMENTAL JOURNEY
## TO MARITAL SUCCESS!

By

*John Curtis, Ph.D.,*

*Fr. Dominic McManus, O.P.,*

*& Mike Day*

NEW PRIORY PRESS

EXPLORING THE DOMINICAN VISION

# TABLE OF CONTENTS

## PREFACE: This Book Is for You

There are a million different reasons you could be reading this book. Maybe it popped up as a seemingly random recommendation from Amazon or you saw a friend post about it on Facebook or Goodreads. Maybe your parish priest or the deacon or sponsor couple helping you with marriage prep is having you read through it before you plan the ceremony. Or maybe your mother slid it across the kitchen table with a knowing look when you finally admitted that you and your girlfriend are sharing an apartment. However you came across this book, there's only one reason to keep reading: it's been written for you.

This book exists because God loves you and His Church cares for you. This book was written because throughout the whole of Church history, but especially for the last thirty years or so, popes, bishops, and theologians from around the world have gone out of their way to teach on the goodness and value of marriage and family life. You are reading this book because the authors have together been so taken with the Church's teaching on marriage and family that they were absolutely compelled to share it—and they have some pretty good ideas on how to make it work for your relationship too—no matter where you've been or where you're at right now.

You are reading this book because God has a mission for you, for your love, and for your marriage. When you professed your vows to your spouse, whether it was 50 years ago or five minutes ago, God gave you a purpose in life—together. If you haven't made those promises yet, then God is even now preparing you to accomplish that purpose, to fulfill that mission. Simply put: the end-all, be-all reason for your life together is to show by your love for one another as husband and wife Christ's love for His Church, God's love for His people, and the greatness to which God really and truly calls each one of us.

Together, you are capable of more, so much more than either of you would be apart. That's the great mission that God is giving you in your relationship. God longs to make both of you saints, and he wants to do so through your spouse; together He wants you to help make saints of all you meet. As a couple you are not just living together to survive, you are being called to thrive. God has brought you together in marriage to succeed; your marriage is called to greatness, and that greatness will be contagious!

If this concept strikes you as odd, you are not alone. "Success" and "greatness" are not terms commonly attributed to marriage today and, unfortunately, what most of society has seen is its failure. Depending upon where you live, your age, and other demographic variables, the odds that your current or future relationship will be successful are only average at best. With such bleak prospects, why even try? Obviously lots of people manage to live relatively happy lives together without trying to get married, so why bother?

One thing is clear: the existing ways of building a relationship do not fully address the realities of love and marriage in the 21$^{st}$ century. The only way a couple can reasonably expect different results is by doing something different. The approach we are proposing is different. It is not foreign and untried but a synthesis of proven business strategies and timeless theological truths.

The union of these two concepts may initially seem strange or paradoxical, especially when applied to love, but this book is all about intimacy. Nothing destroys a loving relationship faster than power struggles, unresolved conflict, feelings of inequity, and the sobering realization that you both have a very different vision for your life together. This book says some unconventional things and says them in a brand new way that you've likely never considered before.

This is an opportunity to discover the inestimable greatness of your calling as a man and woman joined together in marriage and to empower yourselves with a plan to make it happen. You can embrace this challenge for your marriage and strive for success in the greatest endeavor you will ever embark upon or you can try the same thing that's been done for decades and expect little more than the same results.

The choice—the mission—is yours.

## Special Considerations before You Begin

Marriage has changed a lot over time and especially in recent years. Not so long ago divorce was a very rare thing; now, it is literally as common as getting married. Likewise, not that long ago more people didn't live together before they got married than did. Today that situation is basically reversed. Nowadays a majority of people will cohabitate, at least for a while, and oftentimes with more than one person. This did not happen suddenly but was a gradual—and frankly understandable—response to the pain experienced from failed marriages. That isn't to say that everyone who cohabitates comes from a broken home or has commitment issues or anything like that, but in the end cohabitation is designed with the hope of protecting you from the fallout of divorce.

If you are not cohabitating, then you are welcome to jump right in to the next chapter and begin *The Mission of Love*. But if you are cohabitating there are situations and concerns unique to your arrangement that are worth discussing between the two of you first. There are many stigmas and misunderstandings surrounding cohabitation and you may be very conflicted yourself; most couples cohabitate with good intentions and it can appear as though the Church is invalidating something good when in essence it is simply trying to help make your relationship even better. We highly encourage you to read the appendix on cohabitation and other considerations at the end of this book first to help you get the most out of these exercises, which will ultimately deepen the bond between you in a way you never imagined: You are taking the first step of an incredible journey!

# INTRODUCTION:  On A Mission From God

*"They're not gonna catch us. We're on a mission from God."*
*— Elwood Blues*

The 1980 classic *The Blues Brothers* follows the exploits of Jake and Elwood Blues, two musicians who are working to put together a reunion concert for their once-famous band. The movie is full of car crashes, explosions, bar fights, and even Illinois Nazis, but through it all the boys persevere. Why? Because they're on a mission—a mission from God. Putting the band back together isn't just a trip down Nostalgia Lane for Jake and Elwood. They have a vision, a goal they're working towards: they're trying to raise money to save the orphanage they grew up in. Putting the band back together and playing music again is the way they mean to achieve that vision. It's their mission in life. This mission gives their lives meaning, a sense of purpose, an identity which governs their relationships, and a goal to work towards both as individuals and as a group. That mission gives the Blues Brothers direction, and since the mission is from God, it gives them the grace to accomplish what they've been given to do.

What a married couple has been given to do is one of the greatest possible gifts. The *Catechism of the Catholic Church,* the Church's official resource for its beliefs, says this:

> The sacrament of Matrimony signifies the union of Christ and the Church. It gives spouses the grace to love each other with the love with which Christ has loved his Church; the grace of the sacrament thus perfects the human love of the spouses, strengthens their indissoluble unity, and sanctifies them on the way to eternal life (*Catholic Church* 1661).

This is not just a single reference in the *Catechism* either; marriage is everywhere in Scripture. Scripture begins with the marriage of Adam and Eve (Gen 2), it ends with the Wedding Feast of the Lamb (Rev

19), and no metaphor is used more frequently in the New Testament to explain Christ's love for us. In fact, the mission and purpose you have been given is most fully understood in perhaps the most misunderstood passage from St. Paul's letter to the Ephesians. The text on its own can make us uncomfortable today but try to look past the language that's tough and see what's really being said:

> Be subordinate to one another out of reverence for Christ. Wives should be subordinate to their husbands as to the Lord. For the husband is head of his wife just as Christ is head of the church, he himself the savior of the body. As the church is subordinate to Christ, so wives should be subordinate to their husbands in everything. Husbands, love your wives, even as Christ loved the church and handed himself over for her to sanctify her, cleansing her by the bath of water with the word, that he might present to himself the church in splendor, without spot or wrinkle or any such thing, that she might be holy and without blemish. So (also) husbands should love their wives as their own bodies. He who loves his wife loves himself. For no one hates his own flesh but rather nourishes and cherishes it, even as Christ does the church, because we are members of his body. 'For this reason a man shall leave (his) father and (his) mother and be joined to his wife, and the two shall become one flesh.' This is a great mystery but I speak in reference to Christ and the church (Eph 5:21-32).

Now it's easy to get caught on the language of submission but that's really to miss the point. St. Ambrose himself realized this, and he was living in a much more patriarchal society than we are.

> "You are not her master but her husband; she was not given to you to be your slave but your wife.... Reciprocate her attentiveness to you and be grateful to her for her love." (St. Ambrose, *Hexameron*, V 7, 19; cf. JP II, *Familiaris Consortio* 25)

The most perfect form of love, the most perfect form of friendship is that found in Christian marriage, because here the very love of Christ for His Church is made manifest in the lives of the faithful.

Did you know that the only place in the New Testament where the word "sacrament" is used is in the passage above? Of course, it's not really the word "sacrament" (which is Latin) but the Greek word from which our word "sacrament" comes: *mysterion*. "This is a great mystery," St. Paul tells us, "but I speak in reference to Christ and the church." This means that the way we come to understand what sacraments are is by looking at the most natural sacrament in the world: marriage.

## Things Seen and Unseen

A very good traditional definition of a sacrament is a visible sign of an invisible reality, instituted by Christ, which gives grace. We may have learned this or something very like it in Catechism class, and probably we tended to think of it as referring mostly to the more "churchy" sacraments like Baptism or Eucharist. Pouring water over a baby's head (or an adult's, for that matter) signifies washing. But the washing which is signified in the pouring turns out to be more interior than exterior, and the washing of the body washes away all our sins.

Of course, sin can only be forgiven by the special grace of God, which is how we know that sacraments give grace. Or we might think of it in terms of Holy Communion. The bread and the wine naturally represent food and drink, and at the priest's word they become something else. They look like they are feeding our bodies but in fact are feeding our souls. But how on earth can this apply to marriage?

This, of course, is to turn the analogy on its head. It was St. Paul who used the word *mysterion* to talk about marriage; in fact, what he used was *mega mysterion*, in Latin *magnum mysterium*, language usually reserved to the mystery of the Incarnation. Jesus Himself is the *magnum mysterium*, the great mystery that is "contained" within the humanity of Christ is the fullness of divinity. So the "sacraments" or "mysteries" are connected to the Incarnation; they make the same "move" and in some way continue the Incarnation's work.

This is the reason that Pope John Paul II called marriage a "natural sacrament." Clearly both of the partners in a marriage are real, true human beings. At the same time, God works through them to make Himself known and present to the other. Husbands come to know God through their wives; wives through their husbands. In the day-to-day, routine, seemingly mundane events of daily life, God makes His presence known. Maybe the better way to say it is that those seemingly mundane, routine tasks are infused with the Holy Spirit. This becomes especially obvious with the birth of children. It's like the love of the couple for one another is so huge that it can't be contained—it actually becomes another person!

Of course, marriage managed to do all of this before the coming of Christ. Even though most marriages were arranged in those days, the couples did tend to come to love one another (at least as much as now), and their love did break forth into a kind of "incarnation" in the birth of their own children. But Jesus did change some things, or maybe made them clearer. Everyone knows that it was Jesus who said that marriages are indissoluble and that divorce is against God's design from the beginning (we will discuss this at length later), but in doing this Jesus was not making life harder or offering a new legal distinction. Rather, He was showing us just what the sign of marriage signified and that really does make all of the difference.

## A Match Made in Heaven (and for Heaven Too!)

Jesus often referred to Himself as the bridegroom (Mk 2:19; Mt 9:15; Mt 25:1-13; Jn 3:29). Who, then, is Jesus' bride? This is why that passage from St. Paul is so important. "This is a great mystery," he says, "but I speak of Christ and the Church." The Church is Christ's bride: each individual, personally, but much more profoundly all of us together. At the same time, St. Paul says that husbands and wives should love and respect one another like Christ and the Church. The reality which Christian marriage signifies, then, and the mystery which it makes present, is that of Christ and the Church. Where the Christian couple is, where the Christian family lives, there is Christ and His Church.

This is why the Second Vatican Council calls the family the "domestic church." It's not like any of us all on our own or even any couple by themselves perfectly represents the Church but by their self-giving love each and every day, by their common life and prayer, by the way in which parents teach their children the Faith and encourage one another to grow in virtue and holiness, there the mystery of Christ's love for the whole Church is made present and manifest. This is especially true of the marriage vows themselves, for when we say "I do" to one another we are saying, in effect, what Christ said at the Last Supper and showed us on the cross: "This is my body which is for you." This is also why healthy sex is so essential to a holy marriage.

The *Catechism of the Catholic Church* has this to say:

> "Just as of old God encountered his people with a covenant of love and fidelity, so our Savior, the spouse of the Church, now encounters Christian spouses through the sacrament of Matrimony." Christ dwells with them, gives them the strength to take up their crosses and so follow him, to rise again after they have fallen, to forgive one another, to bear one another's burdens, to "be subject to one another out of reverence for Christ," and to love one another with supernatural, tender, and fruitful love. In the joys of their love and family life he gives them here on earth a foretaste of the wedding feast of the Lamb...(*Catholic Church* 1642).

Just as the Eucharist not only makes Christ present now but also gives us a foretaste or a "teaser" of the banquet yet to come, so also marriage gives us, in relationship, the best sense of what life and love in heaven will be like. This is true not just among the married. There in heaven we will all be married, not to one other, but to Christ.

## Called by Name

We tend to think of the word "vocation" simply in terms of vocations to the priesthood or religious life but this is far too small a definition for so great an idea. "Vocation" simply means "calling" from the Latin, *vocare*, that is, "to call." God calls us all to many things. He calls us, He draws us, He instructs us, and He forms us: in His law, according to the virtues, to faith in Christ Jesus, and to life in the Church. This is what the Church at Vatican II called the "universal call" or the "universal vocation" to holiness. Everyone is called to be holy. God wants everyone to wind up a saint.

But God does not call everyone to this holiness in the same way and no one is called to a vocation generically. God doesn't draw anyone to the priesthood in general or religious life non-specifically. Instead, one is called to the priesthood in a particular diocese (like a province in the Church), or in a particular community. Likewise no one is just drawn to religious life as such, but rather is called to life in this community with these particular people. If this is true for priesthood and religious life, which are inherently more "institutional" ways of life, how much more is it true of Christian marriage? No one is "called to marriage" properly speaking; rather, one is called to be married to *this* person. The whole point is that the particular complex of virtues and vices, emotional credits and deficits, and personal strengths and weaknesses are perfectly suited to help and form the other. "The vocation to marriage is written in the very nature of man and woman as they came from the hand of the Creator," (*Catholic Church* 1603). So while the vocation to marriage is generally implicit in each person, God always calls us to it in a specific way, to a particular person, at a particular time.

So Christians are really the first Romantics (recall that the word "romance" comes from "Roman"). It's not that we're especially mushy or that we think that our emotions should rule us at the end of the day, but we do see a place for the emotions in the shared life and love in marriage and we actually have a better case for true love and "happily ever after" than the fairy tales do. The truth we tell in fairy tales is ultimately the truth we live in a Christian marriage; it's the kind of love that moves mountains and splits seas, the hard, deep, powerful sort of love that raises even the dead to life again.

## A Hard Sell

Of course this is all easier said than done. Marriage is a hard sell these days. Relationships fall apart left and right. Relationship columns in newspapers and magazines are just as likely to answer questions about breakups and divorce as they are to answer questions about marriage and commitment. And we all know that more people live together before they're married than don't anymore. Most of these couples report that they're just trying to be "sure" of the relationship before they commit absolutely.

And in some ways who could blame them? Please don't misunderstand: the Church is opposed to cohabitation for some pretty solid reasons, but couples in their twenties and thirties have been seriously scarred, both by the culture and by personal experience, when it comes to marriage. Theirs was the first generation in which as many marriages failed as succeeded. Theirs were the parents who exemplified the most instability of any in history. And they were the children who suffered through the courts and society working out what is just concerning things like child support, custody rights, and visitation. Having seen what happens when marriages break up, having lived firsthand the dangers of a failed relationship and suffered all the ramifications of that failure, who in their right mind would be eager to try it themselves?

This is why good Christian couples are so terribly important. It's why marriages, good, faithful, committed marriages, are the best witness we Christians can offer to the rest of the world about what's really possible. Most couples don't cohabitate indefinitely; they either marry and permanently commit to each other or move on. That's no accident. The imitation is never as good as the original. Whatever attracts you to the copy will eventually stir up a desire for the authentic. But commitment is scary. It's not possible without faith, at least faith in the other person, and probably faith in something else too. Fortunately for us we know in **Whom** we ought to put our *unfailing* trust. *The Catechism* recognizes this fear and also the response:

This unequivocal insistence on the indissolubility of the marriage bond may have left some perplexed and could seem to be a demand impossible to realize. However, Jesus has not placed on spouses a burden impossible to bear, or too heavy—heavier than the Law of Moses. By coming to restore the original order of creation disturbed by sin, he himself gives the strength and grace to live marriage in the new dimension of the Reign of God. It is by following Christ, renouncing themselves, and taking up their crosses that spouses will be able to "receive" the original meaning of marriage and live it with the help of Christ. This grace of Christian marriage is a fruit of Christ's cross, the source of all Christian life (*Catholic Church* 1615).

So it is all a bit like a fairy tale, inasmuch as there's a curse which has skewed our vision. The cross is like Prince Charming's kiss: it breaks the curse and lets us see things aright.

## A High Calling

So what is the right vision of marriage? Well, Jesus proposes this:

Have you not read that from the beginning the Creator 'made them male and female' and said, 'For this reason a man shall leave his father and mother and be joined to his wife, and the two shall become one flesh'? So they are no longer two but one flesh. Therefore, what God has joined together, no human being must separate (Mt 19:5-6).

God has a plan for your marriage. From the dawn of creation He has made us for each other, and the gift that we give of ourselves to each other is total, fruitful, and faithful.

But as with all things, Jesus does more than simply restore what was lost with sin.

Spouses are therefore the permanent reminder to the Church of what happened on the Cross; they are for one another and for their children witnesses to the salvation in which the sacrament makes them sharers. Of this salvation every marriage, like every sacrament, is a memorial, actuation and prophecy: "As a memorial, the sacrament gives them the grace and duty of commemorating the great works of God and of bearing witness to them before their children. As actuation, it gives them the grace and duty of putting into practice in the present, towards each other and their children, the demands of a love which forgives and redeems. As prophecy, it gives them the grace and duty of living and bearing witness to the hope of the future encounter with Christ (*Familiaris consortio*, 13).

Simply put, spouses help to save one another, and they raise up children, not only for the sake of the family or the name but also for the good of the Church and the whole world. Christian spouses are one another's last, best chance of getting to heaven. They're also the ones responsible for the formation of their children, not only in life but also in the Faith. Christian spouses are the representatives of the Church to the world and the sacramental sign, both to each other and to everyone they meet, that Jesus has died for their sins and that everything, absolutely everything, is now different.

*The Mission of Love*, then, understands marriage first and foremost as a vocation rooted in purpose. Your ultimate joy and fulfillment as a married couple will depend upon your commitment to this purpose.

This should come as no surprise, however. We are, after all, purpose-oriented beings. In fact, the human condition can be reduced to three simple questions: 1) Who am I? 2) Where am I going? and 3) Why? Every emotional struggle in your life is the result of a conflict with or an inability to answer one of these three questions. As a man and woman, both with a unique purpose ingrained within them as individuals, come into union, the state of their relationship will depend on their ability to address these same three questions: 1) Who are we? 2) Where are we going? and 3) Why?

Second, *The Mission of Love* emphasizes the necessity of planning. As Benjamin Franklin is often quoted as saying, "Those who fail to plan, plan to fail." It is not enough to recognize our purpose; we must create the means necessary to accomplish it. For example, just as successful businesses and organizations are grounded in established principles and sound practices, so too is the love of Christ ordered towards the fulfillment of His mission. With the concepts and activities in this book, you will be able to create and define "us," who you are together as a couple. It will still be important for you, as a couple, to understand the "blueprint" for marriage by learning the theology behind your sacrament because it will aid the development of your vision for your life together and how it is lived. It is also crucial that you become your own "mechanics" by learning effective tools for communication and conflict resolution to assist with the process of developing objectives for your relationship and dealing with any conflicts that arise through this process of growth. But these are not the focus of this book. *The Mission of Love* is that critical first task of laying a foundation upon which the rest of your married life will be built.

In addition, concepts and activities in this book are not for one audience alone: they can be successfully applied to a budding romance or a new marriage or to validate and strengthen a relationship that has already lasted decades. The Chapter Objectives which are listed at the head of each chapter, as well as the Recap which is listed at the end will help you to focus on those portions of the book which have the most bearing on you and your partner in your situation. This book can even provide answers about why previous relationships failed and how your experience of those setbacks can actually improve your judgment in making better relationship choices now. The Mission model is truly simple and straightforward but be warned—applying it to your relationship may not be easy and may even be unsettling at times. But the activities in this book can also be fun and energizing, as you and your partner embark on this process of self-discovery and explore various aspects of your relationship. Enjoy the journey, and be ready for the best of surprises!

# CHAPTER 2

# BOOK I: Who Are We?

One of the toughest shifts newly married couples have to struggle with is moving from an "I" mentality to a "We" mentality. It's not generally a conscious thing but it is very hard to go from thinking about "She and I" or "He and I" to "us." Yet in the friendship of marriage the individual "I"s do, in a certain way, yield to the collective "us." Karol Wojtyla, who later became Pope John Paul II, put it this way:

> The essence of betrothed [marital] love is self-giving, the surrender of one's 'I'. This is something different from and more than attraction, desire, or even goodwill...When betrothed love enters into this interpersonal relationship something more than friendship results:

> Two people give themselves each to the other...The fullest, the most uncompromising form of love consists precisely in self-giving, in making one's inalienable and non-transferable 'I' someone else's property. This is doubly paradoxical: firstly in that it is possible to step outside one's own 'I' in this way, and secondly in that the 'I' far from being destroyed or impaired as a result is enlarged and enriched (Karol Wojtyla, *Love and Responsibility*, 2: 96-97).

We find ourselves in giving ourselves away, even as Jesus said: "Whoever wants to find his life will lose it" (Mt 16:25). In Christian marriage we give ourselves wholly over to the other, even as the other does for us. In this mutual and reciprocal self-giving something new and wonderful happens, and this is the birth of the "We" or the "Us."

In fact, we can see this truth most tangibly in that greatest gift of marital love: the miracle of human life. Through the union of a man and woman, their love calls into existence a human being that is neither just the man nor just the woman but a new life that is their very love, together, personified. It is their "us," their one flesh, quite literally.

Now each partner is already an unrepeatable and unique person and so that act of self-donation and reception of another altogether unique person results in literally an infinite variety of "We's." This new "We" will not make you both less yourselves but more. The "you" that you are together will be more than either of you could ever have been on your own. But finding and naming and articulating this new "We" is very hard work. Much of this is not very conscious. It's the normal work of dating and courtship and getting to know one another. Part of the reason for an engagement is precisely to give the couple the freedom to engage this dynamic without the pressure of still constantly trying to have to woo their partner. Of course this work is never done but certainly by the time of the wedding a couple should have a reasonable enough idea of who "they" are together as a unit as opposed to two disparate individuals. The following chapters focus on shifting your focus from "I" to "us." They are meant to take your interior vision, reveal it to one another, and help you create a shared vision that is neither one nor the other but something altogether unique to who the two of you are together.

# CHAPTER 1:
## Creating the Vision of Your Relationship Together

*"The best way to plan for the future is to create it"*
*— Peter Drucker*

**Chapter Objectives**

- Come up with a Vision Statement for your marriage, both individually and together.
- Learn new ways to listen to your partner.
- Develop negotiation techniques which will help you navigate conflicts in your relationship.

The foundation of marriage is choice: it is an act of free will to swear the whole of your life to another until death do you part. This is no minor promise; it will come to define who you are for the rest of your life through every struggle, endeavor, or accomplishment in a way that nothing else can. With a commitment as potent and life-changing as marriage, it is quite amazing how many otherwise intelligent people just assume that somehow something this important will magically work itself out.

Often couples simply "wing it" as they move through the commonly assumed phases of any long-term, intimate relationship, starting with romance, then followed by commitment, which is a prelude for the predictable conflict phase. Then, if they are fortunate enough to successfully make it through the turmoil of the conflict phase, they may achieve true and authentic intimacy… where they know everything about their partner but still love them anyway!

This is a frequent issue for couples who have been married for a moderate period of time (say, 3-10 years). Even though the couple has known each other for a long while, they have more or less taken their relationship step by step and have never created a shared, long-term vision for their future together. If there is not a shared vision for the relationship, a common purpose that unites them, each will default towards pursuing their own individual purposes. If this continues long enough, there may come a moment when their individual paths have drifted so far apart that they no longer know who they are anymore— or worse, demean and resent the other because they've become an obstacle to their own individual path. This turns the proverbial molehill into a mountain, and makes a mushroom cloud out of what started as a small campfire.

So, one of the best things you can do for your marriage and future family life is to come up with a shared Vision Statement. At first this might seem counterintuitive, or even silly, but think about the marriages and relationships you know of which have failed. What are the major causes? Chores, Kids, Money? Sex? Time? Work? For example: *She spends too much money. He can't save for anything. He wants sex all the time. She never wants to be with me. He never lifts a finger around the house. He thinks his job is more important than mine. She works all of the time and never makes any space for me. She lets the kids walk all over her.* What are these but misplaced expectations? How could this have been better avoided than with a common shared vision of the future ideal state of the marriage?

Think of the Vision Statement for your marriage the way some people post inspirational notes on their bathroom mirror or one of those quote posters you might keep on your desk at work. There is no right way to do this. It could be short or long, detailed or sketchy, containing a list with bullets or embedded in prose. The point is finding out a way to say what you and your partner want for your common life together. What does the future ideal state "look like"? One where you support one another? Where the relationship is harmonious and free of conflict? How do you think of yourselves together? What kind of a couple are you? What would be your ideal way of relating to one another? How will you relate, both as individuals and as a couple, to other people? What is it you mean to do together? How do you hope to get there?

# Articulating the Vision of Your Marriage

Depending upon where you work you may or may not have a Vision Statement prominently displayed somewhere in your office, lobby, or on the website. It offers a description of the future ideal state of the organization. It often expresses in bold and poetic terms the values which the company's owners or shareholders hold dear and the basic expectations which management, employees, and customers may share. Vision Statements are idealistic on purpose. They hold up the model, the ideal, the possibility of just what can be.

If you've ever been part of writing a Vision Statement, either at work or in some other organization, one of the major problems is that the whole statement is itself typically produced by a committee. This is a terrible misunderstanding of equality. If your marriage teaches you anything let it be that while both parties certainly have to give up certain hopes and dreams, preferences and desires, it also means they have to share them.

Practically speaking this means that when you go to write down a Vision Statement you should start it as a solo project. You can do this at church or at home but either way, start in different physical locations.

Perhaps a good time would actually be during a time when you are used to being alone. Maybe you could work on your Vision Statement when your partner is at the gym, and then your spouse could work on theirs when you are out running errands. The point is to give yourself real time and real space so that you don't feel pressed in any way by your partner. This initial attempt is as much for you as it is for them. And don't worry, they'll have their chance too. Marriage is a total gift of yourself to the other so the best thing that you can do for your partner is simply to be yourself.

So sit somewhere by yourself, perhaps with a picture of the two of you, and pray. Ask God to help you best understand what He's asking of the both of you, as individuals and as a couple. Then consider some of your best times together. These might be weekend getaways or a particularly memorable date. It might be the day of a proposal or the evening of your wedding. Or it might be the rock she was for you when your father died or the way she helped you recover from that hiking accident. The point is you want at the front of your mind what you as a couple are when you are at your best together.

Now just start to write. Don't worry about grammar or punctuation or how good any of it is going to sound. Just come up with adjectives to describe not only how you felt when you were with your partner at these key moments but how you were together. Come up with an image or two that symbolizes or otherwise resonates with you in thinking of your relationship. Start combining these ideas and see what comes together— you might just be surprised!

Eventually you'll want to work your ideas into a few sentences of prose, or at least a bulleted list of ideas or characteristics. This may take several attempts. People often find themselves dealing with some pretty serious emotions when initially attempting the exercise, especially if there are significant places in the relationship where you and your partner are not on the same page. Give yourself and your partner some time. Establish a two- or three-week deadline for getting this initial stage done.

## Vision Statement Mash-Up

Now comes the next challenge. Block out a significant period of time, at least an hour or two, to go over your individual statements together. Remember, just as this exercise may have begun to stir up some things emotionally for you, it likely did the same thing for your partner. Be very kind and tread very carefully.

One common technique priests and deacons use in marriage pre-paration is to ask in the course of an interview two separate questions: Are you sexually active and if so how frequently? Later on in the interview the question is then asked: Do you pray together, and if so how frequently? Perhaps not surprisingly, it is easier for most people to sleep with somebody than to pray with them. When surveyed about why they don't pray together the number one reason given by couples is that prayer is too intimate. Because of our fallen nature, there is not always intimacy in sex. But when we open ourselves and share with another the depths of our soul to be received just as openly by another it creates an immensely powerful bond.

This exercise will require a great deal of intimacy and you may find it difficult to do. Sharing needs to be approached with great care. Expressing one's hopes and dreams, fears and failings, visions for the future and worries over the past is a tender thing and there is always the risk of being rejected, dismissed, or ignored. DO NOT IGNORE ANYTHING THAT YOUR PARTNER HAS TO SAY. You may not ultimately wind up agreeing on it but take it seriously. If they've elected to share it with you it's because it is important to them, and that, all by itself, should make it important to you.

There's no right way to proceed but there are any number of wrong ways to continue the conversation. It is probably best if initially one partner shares their statement and the other simply listens. After a time the receiving partner might want to offer some supportive comments and highlight the portions with which they feel they best connect. Then have the other partner share their statement and repeat the process. Only after both partners have shared their project and received some positive feedback should things continue.

## From Two to One

The goal of the exercise is to help us move from a solitary vision of your future to a shared one and to develop a common vision that is truly "ours," and not just "yours" or "mine" imposed on the other.

Most people have a very hard time actually saying what they want. Many of us, even in relatively healthy relationships, have a tendency to give in to the will of the other so as to avoid conflict and arguments. It's a bad habit in a relationship and ultimately can result in damaging or even destroying a marriage. If one person constantly makes all of the decisions, and the other person is constantly having to simply follow the will of the other, then resentment is inevitable and it prevents any true equality in the relationship.

Many of the exercises in this book require a certain amount of emotional intimacy and open the potential for conflict. This is because coming to share a common vision is one of the hardest parts of a marriage. The idea is not to start a fight but rather to provide you a safe space in which to negotiate the conflicts which already exist in this intimate relationship. By doing so, you will come to a stronger depth of commitment and sense not only of self but of a common identity as a couple.

This is where married people can take a page from the playbook of consecrated religious. The *Rule* of St. Augustine begins, "The first reason you have come into the house [monastery], brothers, is that you should be of one heart and one mind on the way to God."(I, 2) Again, the vision of any Christian marriage is going to be rooted absolutely in the overall vision of any Christian; namely, the universal call to holiness and the evangelization of the world. That is, any particular value or goal needs to be assessed in light of the overall commitment which has grounded you both in Christ.

## Negotiation

One of the key components to navigating the conflict of differing visions is negotiation. It's a critical relationship skill to have in general and absolutely essential to arriving at a common vision. Don't be fooled: you and your partner already have a great deal in common and, naturally, you already hold common values and ideals. That's part of what attracted you to one another in the first place. But another important part of what makes couples better are the differences that exist between them. Marriage is not about validating what you already know to be true about yourself, it's about becoming the person you could never have become without your spouse. We grow in patience and charity by learning to tolerate one another's quirks and difficulties, and our partners help us to expand our horizons and see the world differently than we did before. What this means is that if it seems like you and your partner already agree on practically everything, scratch just a little bit deeper; what's underneath is worth exploring.

The first secret to good negotiation is recognizing where the conflicts actually lie. Once you start going through both Vision Statements line by line, don't look so much for verbatim agreement but common themes and ideas. He may talk about living with integrity and she may talk about honesty. These aren't radically different concepts but the difference in words could drive some people crazy. She might talk about financial responsibility and he might talk about personal security. As you go through, identify those points of commonality and try to develop those parts of your common statement first. Only then return to the thornier issues after you've proven to yourself and to each other that you can handle conflict together.

Once you determine actual points of conflict the most important thing is to stay in the conversation. It's awkward, it's uncomfortable, you might say things you don't quite mean to, or say things that you mean but that you've never had the courage to say, and yes, feelings can get hurt. Some pain is inevitable in any relationship that goes beyond the surface, but staying in the conversation ensures that the pain is not in vain. A wise old priest once said, "If you come down from the cross, you never experience the joy of the resurrection." Suffering through this together will help you to draw closer, and by the time it's done it will become clear that the task wasn't as awful as it seemed at times in the heat of the moment.

The other thing to remember—and this can't be emphasized enough—is that the goal is not to win. That's probably the only way to fail in this exercise. The purpose in arriving at a common vision of the future ideal state of your marriage is to come to understand better the values which you hold in common and the kinds of goals to which those values move you. What this means is that if you see something as really essential to your relationship, and your partner could take it or leave it, then you need to find a way to articulate why that is so important and talk with your partner about why it doesn't seem as important to them. Very likely you will both come to realize certain values that you do not share, or maybe certain values which you do share but which had been less clear before your partner explained it. When that happens be sure to thank each other for having helped you to understand something new.

Finally, there will inevitably be things about which you actually disagree. That's fine. Not everything needs to go into a Vision Statement and not everything needs to be agreed upon in a marriage. The important thing is to be clear with one another about what you actually think. This takes great trust because you are essentially saying, "I love you more than anything but I really disagree on this one," and still trusting the other to love you back. Done correctly, this will dramatically strengthen your marriage and over time will increase your love for each other. Just be clear about the disagreements and how you agree to live with them.

## Writing Our Vision Statement

Having identified the key elements of your common vision, it's now time to start writing. Sometimes it's helpful to do this over more than one session, especially if writing down values, feelings, and essential components was an unsettling emotional exercise. Other times, if the energy seems really to be flowing, it's worth it to take a break and come back a few days later. In any case, give yourself time with the whole exercise and let the insights percolate a little bit before you try to use them too directly.

Sometimes it's helpful to start with one of the images that you came up with, either alone or together. Other times one central idea gets the ball rolling. Either way, articulating a clear, common vision in a single sentence or two, which roots your marriage in your common vocation to grow in holiness and become better people, is an essential starting point. The rest of the statement could remain in bulleted form or could be written in prose. If you are so inclined it could even be written in verse. The point is that together you now describe in words the future ideal state of your marriage which you can both authentically sign on to and be happy with.

Listen closely to each other and play to one another's strengths. If she's the better writer then let her do the actual writing but stay engaged the whole way through to show your continued interest and investment. If he's the finer wordsmith then give him space to work his magic and compliment the parts you like best. Don't be afraid to express concern, reservation, or disagreement. Stay with it until it's done and when you're both satisfied print it out and sign it together at the bottom. Post it somewhere prominent where you can both see it. Some couples find reciting their Vision Statement, either alone or together, to be a helpful activity. Others find returning to it periodically to see how they're matching up to be useful. Still others find that, given a little more time, the statement itself needs revising. The important thing is to have it and to continue to articulate to the other the common vision that you have for your life together and how you mean to get there. If you keep that up no grace will pass you by in your marriage and the overall vision which you have both been given, to help each other become the people you were always meant to be, is the one thing you can be sure of.

The pages which follow provide some resources designed to help you write your Vision Statement. Use them as you find them helpful but if some other format appeals to you more then go with that. The important thing is that the end-product is meaningfully *yours*—together.

## Getting Started - "Warm-Up" Exercises

### Exercise #1

Before you begin writing a Vision Statement, you might want to do a little pre-work. You may want to identify some of your core values to incorporate into your statement. One way to spot these is to look for tangible items in your life that represent the things you value most: maybe a piece of jewelry you're wearing, an emblem on your key chain, a picture on your computer desktop, or a cherished symbol on the wall. Typically, these items remind you of something of great value to you—a religious icon, a beloved grandparent, a significant life accomplishment, and so on. A Vision Statement for your relationship might incorporate these core values and you may find it easier to begin writing your vision once you have pinpointed tangible items that you treasure.

## Exercise #2

Consider doing a search on the Internet for other examples of Vision Statements. Go to websites of organizations that you know and trust. Consider the website of your employer or your place of worship, a community hospital, your favorite electronics brand, your alma mater, or even a branch of local or state government. Many examples are readily available and viewing how others have written Vision Statements may help you develop a better one for your relationship.

## Vision Statement Examples

Look at the following examples of two seemingly different Vision Statements from the same couple. Each partner created the statement separately.

## Hers:

In our ideal life, we will express our individuality through our intelligence and creativity. We are equal partners in our relationship but value each other's different approach to life. We are close to God and active in our Church. We do all this with the intention of being truthful with each other and ourselves and by enriching our lives and leaving the world a better place. We will travel, expand our horizons, deepen family relationships, and live life to the fullest, free of materialistic burdens.

## His:

My vision for the future ideal state of our relationship is one based on integrity and full of rich and deep meaning that comes from ever-increasing exploration of who we are and how we show our love. We each will be devoted to helping the other reach their full potential. We will give our children roots and wings, and always laugh and learn with them. We will achieve financial serenity and maintain balance in all areas of life together.

You can see that the couple has different perspectives but once they share and integrate their visions, they may be closer in meaning than they seem. Look for the commonalities in concepts and values, regardless of the words. Are you using terms that sound different on the surface but are really saying the same basic thing? You may be talking about the value of "integrity" while your partner emphasizes "truth." Can you see how they are similar and resolvable when examined side by side? When you identify core concepts and values within each Vision Statement, you might find that you are closer to each other than you thought.

Also, don't be concerned if your Vision Statements sound completely different from these examples. There is no right way to do this and no predetermined outcome. The key is to be bold, honest, creative, and future-focused with an emphasis on the ideal state you desire for the relationship.

## Combining Your Vision Statements

This part of the activity is similar to lighting a unity candle at a wedding ceremony (this is not really a Catholic ritual but many priests tolerate it and it can be useful for our purposes here). It starts out with each partner lighting an individual candle, then taking two separate flames and making them one.

This is a symbol of joining your individual visions into one common vision for the relationship.

# CHAPTER 2:
## What Do We Stand For?
## Branding Your Relationship

*"Here I am my friend and me, here we are not two but three:*
*he and me and He." – St. Aelred of Rievaulx*

St. Aelred was a monk who lived in the eleventh century in England. He wrote a little book called *Spiritual Friendship* which is one of the first and, to this day, one of the best things ever written explicitly on friendship in the Christian tradition. He sees friendship as a kind of natural sacrament whereby, in the other who is made in the image and likeness of God, we, who are also the same image and likeness, come to encounter God and come to see ourselves as we really are. Christian friendship, he says, is that and then some. Christian friendship not only reveals the divine on a natural level but is at the same time itself enlivened by grace. The Christian friendship itself becomes a kind of mini-Trinity: she and me and He. Aelred taught this, at least in part, because certain strains of the monastic tradition were very suspicious of friendship. He made the following clear: God is present even in purely human friendships, so friendship among Christians is not only permissible but to be fostered as one of the best aids to the spiritual life, and that certain kinds of friendship (marriage and religious life) are actually ordered to one another's salvation.

## Chapter Objectives
- Identify 3 signs or symbols which are important to each of you, perhaps outside of the immediate context of your relationship.
- Identify at least 3 symbols which each of you feels represents your vision for your relationship.
- Identify at least 3 mottos, sayings, or quotations which say something important to you about marriage.

Now we live in an age that, because of certain romantic ideals, already presumes friendship as integral to marriage. This hasn't been the case for much of human history. Cicero wrote one of the first great books on friendship and Aristotle and Plato both talk about it as well. None of them think friendship is meaningfully possible in marriage. Why? Because friendship has to be between people who are, at least on a certain level, equals. They simply didn't believe that women were equal to men. Very early on, however, Christians began to question such a position. St. Paul gestures towards it in that fifth chapter of the Letter to the Ephesians. A number of the Fathers of the Church at least reference it, including St. Augustine. But perhaps the most perfect synthesis is that of St. Thomas Aquinas:

> The greater that friendship is, the more solid and long-lasting will it be. Now, there seems to be the greatest friendship [*maxima amicitia*] between husband and wife, for they are united not only in the act of fleshly union, which produces a certain gentle association even between animals but also in the partnership of the whole range of domestic activity. Consequently, as an indication of this, man must even 'leave his father and mother' for the sake of his wife, as is said in Genesis (2:24) (*SCG* 3:123,6).

You see, not only is friendship possible in marriage but marriage itself is meant to be the greatest friendship, the *amicitia maxima*. How? Because of what St. Aelred said above. Because in the marriage the two individuals become something new, something one, something other. The two become one flesh, not only or even mostly in sexual union, though that is perhaps the greatest physical sign of what is happening interiorly. No, the man leaves his father and mother, and the woman hers, in order to cling to one another, going from two individual "I's" to a collective "We."

## A Sacramental Symbol

Our world is dominated by signs and symbols for everything. Signs tell us where we are, where we're going, and what's there once we arrive. Symbols tell us many of the same things but they also solicit something more from us. They begin to communicate something of the reality that they represent. They stir up our hearts and generate an emotional and sometimes even a spiritual response. Sacraments are something different still. They are both signs and symbols but they are also something more. baptism is clearly about washing away sin and guilt. Holy water is a symbol which represents this but baptism actually does it: when someone pours water over a person who has not been baptized and says, "I baptize you in the name of the Father, and of the Son, and of the Holy Spirit," the person really is baptized, forgiven, and made new.

The Church insists that marriage is a sacrament but a sacrament of what? The other sacraments are fairly obvious: Baptism is about forgiveness of sins and entry into the Church, Confirmation about the gift of the Holy Spirit, Eucharist about the enduring Presence of Christ's sacrifice, Reconciliation about forgiveness of sins after baptism, Anointing of the Sick about healing and strength, and Holy Orders about ordering the work of the Church. But what is marriage a sign of and what reality does it communicate?

The *Catechism of the Catholic Church* (1661) says this:

> The sacrament of Matrimony signifies the union of Christ and the Church. It gives spouses the grace to love each other with the love with which Christ has loved his Church; the grace of the sacrament thus perfects the human love of the spouses, strengthens their indissoluble unity, and sanctifies them on the way to eternal life (cf. Council of Trent: DS 1799).

On a purely natural level, spouses are fulfilling their basic life's duty simply by getting married, living as married people, and potentially having children. This is in obedience to the "first command" of the law: Be fruitful and multiply (Gen 1:28). On a supernatural level, a sacramental marriage between two Christians united in faith and baptism is graced also to stand for and make present a deeper reality still: the love of Christ for His Church—that is, true and perfect love.

All sacraments have signs and symbols associated with them that communicate and dispose us to their reception. As we said before, holy water reminds us of baptism even when no one is being baptized. A purple stole or a confessional box puts us all in the mind of considering our sins. A Roman collar signifies ordination. A vial of oil suggests anointing. But what about marriage? What is the most visible sign that makes up the Sacrament of Matrimony?

The rings. The ring or rings (there are some places in the world where only the bride receives the ring; this dates mostly from a time when a man's ring was a symbol of authority—like the bishop's) are blessed in the wedding ceremony by the priest or deacon, and then the rings are exchanged by the couple with the following formula "Take this ring as a sign of my love and fidelity, in the name of the Father, and of the Son, and of the Holy Spirit." For most people wedding bands are important symbols of their marriage in general, but for Christians they are "sacramentals" just as surely as holy water, rosaries, and medals of saints.

Think about that as you consider symbols for your own marriage. Symbols don't have to be complex in order to be powerful; in fact, some of the most powerful symbols are also the simplest. Just think of what Jesus used: water, oil, bread, wine, and the touch of a hand. These simplest of signs communicate actual grace, make God tangibly present, and give us a living share in the life of God. Of course, these signs don't make God present all by themselves. It is by the power of the Holy Spirit given to the Church that these natural signs are transformed into something more. You too are the same. You are natural symbols of love but by God's grace and the gift of the Holy Spirit you are made to represent, to communicate, and to make present something more. As symbols of God's love you will make manifest the love of Christ for His Church but as living recipients of the ongoing Sacrament of Matrimony you will make present that love throughout your married lives, much as the priests make Christ present through the ongoing effects of the Sacrament of Holy Orders. This is why the Church takes marriage so seriously; you, too, hold a high office essential and necessary to the Church.

## Branding

Creating a common symbol for your life together, "branding" your marriage, is an important complement to your Vision Statement. In the New Testament the Greek word for "brand" is used for the cross in the Book of Revelation: those who are saved are marked on their foreheads with a sign indicating to Whom they belong.

Most of us do the same thing today. Our clothes are all marked: with a Nike swoosh, with a Ralph Lauren polo horse and rider, or our favorite team or school mascot. Sometimes we didn't even go to the school and never played for the team but because we are fans we want to be associated with them. And, as creatures of habit and as loyal customers, we mostly wear the same stuff all of the time. So some guys always wear Dockers, some gals always have Uggs boots, and so on. The "brand" both marks the clothes and the wearer. This is why it is important to choose wisely what we wear and which brands we choose to associate ourselves with.

Branding is important because it can often communicate something about the organization which is less than obvious. For instance, everyone recognizes the polo shirts with the alligator on them: they're Lacoste. But what few people know is that the alligator is a reference to Rene Lacoste, the founder of the company. He was so tenacious on the tennis court that he was nicknamed "the Crocodile." Not only did the image become synonymous with comfortable shirts but it also came to represent Lacoste's vision and business model which was equally tenacious.

It's going to be important for you to similarly "brand" yourselves as a married couple with symbolism that you believe represents who you are and the vision for your lives together. The point here is not so much to say, "Look at us. Isn't our marriage great?" It's more about saying, "This is what we stand for as a couple. These are our ideals and our hopes and our dreams made concrete. What does this stir up in you?" Nothing helps married couples like the witness and support of already married couples, whether those are families, friends, or acquaintances from work, church, or elsewhere. It's certainly true that whatever "brand" you come up with might not be used publicly or regularly but, as with the Vision Statement, it can be a valuable resource for you to return to as a couple to see how you're measuring up to your agreed-upon ideals. We have a sample exercise at the end of this chapter which helps to guide you through the process of coming up with your own brand, but first it might be helpful to consider just how symbols work.

Sometimes the Vision Statement helps to name the abstract ideals but lacks a certain concrete element. If one of you is a more abstract thinker and the other is more image-oriented, this exercise can prove especially valuable. You can use it to come up with any sort of symbol which can bear the weight of the ideals which you're putting behind it, but we've arranged it in the way we have for a reason.

## Coat of Arms

Coats of Arms have been symbolic of families and individuals for more than a thousand years. Originally they were draped across shields to be taken into battle, just as the ancient Romans used a kind of logo on their shields identifying whichever unit they belonged to. Over time, however, their actual military use gave way to a kind of personal branding. In the Church, individual bishops, cardinals, and popes are all invited to create their own arms. In addition, they pick a motto which runs along the bottom of the shield which is meant to summarize their personal philosophy or sense of purpose. That's the kind of thing we'd like for you to come up with.

Start by going online. There are dozens of heraldry websites that discuss how coats of arms came to be, how to use them and such but what you're most interested in is what the symbols typically mean. They'll have sample shields there, maybe even one with your surname. Look it up. Also look up your high school or college's coat of arms – they've almost certainly got one too. Just snoop around and get to know basically what they look like, what symbols are attractive to you, and maybe get an idea for some mottos.

Over the next couple of days keep your eyes open: reading the paper, flipping through old magazines, watching TV, searching the web; look for signs, symbols, or logos that seem to resonate with what you wrote in your Vision Statement.

If you still have the sheet that you first used to brainstorm for the Vision Statement, return to that and see what were some of the single-word descriptions you used to come up with the longer form. Feel free to mark things down or cut them up as you go. Then pick a time, say within a week of having started the project, and bring all of your stuff together. Show one another the symbols you came up with and talk about why they are important to you. Remember, just as when you wrote the Vision Statement, these are deeply personal realities to your partner; if you don't understand something say so respectfully.

If one of you is artistic you may simply wish to draw this on your own. If not you may want to cut and paste, both figuratively with images online or literally with newspaper or magazine clippings. If you're more technologically inclined we do have a blank template available online for a free download. Begin to fill it in. Play with this for a while. See what fits and what doesn't. Discuss the symbols and make clear to each other why certain ones are so important for you.

Once the image is finished take some time to look at it together. Talk about what you like about it. Discuss ways in which you see the ideals embodied there present in your relationship. Commit yourselves to living them both better. Now start playing with the motto. It should be short, pithy, and clear; but most importantly, it should clearly represent you two as a couple. One of you may be very brave and the other one not especially so: "Courage" is, in that case, probably not a great idea for you. But if you both have had to overcome great adversity, especially together, then maybe "Courage," is fine, or perhaps, "Never give up. Never give in." It doesn't matter where they come from. It could be a favorite movie quote or a short passage from a book. It could just be a set phrase you two use together a lot. When you find something that you can both agree on write it down.

Now hang the coat of arms somewhere you both can see it: in the bathroom, the bedroom, hallway, or on the fridge. Look at it every day and let it remind you of what you mean to one another. Talk about it at times and how you try to live up to it. Maybe post it with your Vision Statement so that you can have a kind of constant reminder of what you've signed up for and what it means.

Just remember: as powerful as this symbol may become for both of you, you are to be an even more powerful symbol for the rest of us. You two are part of a living sacrament, a sign which continues and which communicates Christ's love for His Church, not only to one another but to everyone you meet.

## Recap

- What signs and symbols did you come up with which identified values which are important to you?
- What signs and symbols were important for each of you in the context of your relationship? What did you learn about each other in reflecting on those symbols?
- What sayings especially struck you, either yours or your partner's?

# CHAPTER 3:
## Growing the Body

*"No man is an island, entire of itself,*
*Each is a piece of the continent, a part of the main..."*
*—John Donne*

Whenever a couple marries two lives merge into one. A "me" quickly gives way to an "us" and an "I" to an "we." Yet the lives which are merged are never simply that of the partners alone. Think of the whole host of new relationships which you have forged with in-laws, relatives, and other friends, all of whom you likely would never have known were it not for your spouse. One of the most important decisions you will ever make in the course of your marriage is when, where, and how to go about forging these new relationships and when to invite new people into the body of your marriage. This chapter will concern itself with the business of growing the body of your marriage—of expanding the outward boundaries of your family through mergers and acquisitions with other individuals and their families.

## Chapter Objectives
- Explore the significant factors which make being a family different today as compared to families in the past.
- Use the categories of "mergers" and "acquisitions" to better understand the dynamics of responsibly growing a family.
- Respectfully appreciate, utilize, and, where appropriate, blend family life and cultures based on differing family histories.
- Discuss the consequences of marrying into a blended family situation and how to establish a new familial identity instead of simply ceding one's own identity to the new family unit.

## Domestic Church

The words from John Donne at the head of the chapter reminds us that no person is complete all by himself and, at the same time, that each person is a kind of microcosm of the whole human race. The

Church is the same even if we don't usually think of it that way. As the Second Vatican Council teaches:

> From the wedlock of Christians there comes the family, in which new citizens of human society are born, who by the grace of the Holy Spirit received in baptism are made children of God, thus perpetuating the people of God through the centuries. The family is, so to speak, the domestic church. In it parents should, by their word and example, be the first preachers of the Faith to their children; they should encourage them in the vocation which is proper to each of them, fostering with special care vocation to a sacred state (*Lumen Gentium*, 11).

Does this mean that we have to sit around reading the Bible all the time, pray seven times a day, and wear funny clothes? No, the Church isn't calling you to be anything other than you are: husband, father, wife, mother, and so on; rather, the Church is trying to show you just how much potential there is in being a husband and father, a wife and a mother. It does mean that prayer needs to be an essential component of your daily life together, probably at morning and in the evening and at least before meals, and we'll help you with that in a later chapter. It also means that some part of your living quarters should be decorated as a sort of sacred space. As kids come along this can become a very helpful way to mark the passing of the seasons. It also means that you have an obligation to set an example for your kids in terms of charitable giving, stewardship of time and example in volunteering.

Your domestic church will draw its life and find its completion in the life of your local parish. Your pastor's priesthood and that of his associates is not in competition with your own but is there to support it. The common prayer you share together as a couple and as a family is fulfilled most perfectly in the Church's liturgy. And how better can you learn what it means to give yourself body and soul to your spouse than by weekly, if not daily, encountering in the most personal way possible the God who says, "This is my body...This is my blood, given up for you"?

Gone are the days when the only expectation of everyday Christians is to pay, pray, and obey. You do need to do all of these things but your life as everyday Catholic Christians will and should change dramatically as you grow into the sacrament of marriage. Of course, the most dramatic growth in your domestic church will always take place by acquiring new members, whether those new members come about as a result of the physical sacrifice of one another's bodies which spouses make together on the marriage bed, or as the result of the generous reception of children or other relatives from a previous relationship or due to special circumstances.

## Mergers and Acquisitions

When businesses talk about two or more companies merging, the hope is that the new whole will be greater and more successful than the sum of its parts. Ideally, two businesses uniting works to create a whole new organization with a fresh identity and culture. This new identity is initially an unrealized ideal but it is an important one because working towards that ideal is in fact the goal of the merger. A healthy merger is all about establishing a partnership in which each participant is given the space, freedom, and resources to grow, gain, and benefit, and most of all to attain a potential they would not have had all on their own.

Mergers in marriage are based on an equal partnership of life and love, even if the partners come into the marriage with an unequal amount of baggage, liability, or assets. Acquisitions are more complicated and occur when a marital merger involves: children, stepchildren, live-in parents, younger siblings (who may or may not be adults yet), family members with special needs, and in-laws..

Marital mergers always involve some measure of acquisition, whether we like it or not; but some kinds of acquisition require a more ready response than others and so must be assessed differently. For instance, whether you wind up joining all of your financial assets or not, your new spouse's debt does meaningfully become your own, at least inasmuch as they are responsible for the debt and therefore can't contribute whatever portion of their salary goes to paying off the previous debt. Children, however, and elderly parents (a growing concern as people marry later in life and as seniors live to older ages) pose a very different challenge.

When businesses deal with a merger or an acquisition there are two major levels of concern. One might be called the structural dimension of the merger. This involves things like the physical building, software systems, equipment, staff, inventory, and so on.

The other is the cultural dimension which, in some ways, is harder to see but includes: patterns of communication, attitudes, morale, values, levels of teamwork, organizational history, workload, satisfaction among workers, and history of change in the company. One of the things which consultants do is assess, through a variety of measures, the "change readiness capabilities" of a particular business. You need to do this too.

As with businesses, most couples focus, especially in the beginning, on the structural components of the marriage: house, furniture, appliances, financial assets, and the like. It is important to take great care with these, but it is equally important, and often much more difficult, to take great care with the cultural components of your marriage: your collective vision, personal objectives and values, hopes and dreams, and all the rest. The way you get to these, no longer alone but now together, involves healthy patterns of communication, negotiation skills, and problem-solving techniques. The way in which you manage both the structural and the cultural will largely determine the quality and success of the marriage merger.

## The Challenge

This all sounds very neat in the abstract, and no doubt you are already putting some of these pieces together in your head, but let's lay out a couple of concrete examples and consider the cultural and structural concerns which will need to be attended to.

Rob and Becky are planning on getting married in six months. They are both twenty-eight years old. Rob has a degree in art history but owns and manages a local gym. Becky is an insurance adjustor who met Rob at the gym. Neither has ever been married before but Becky has a child from a previous relationship, a six-year-old girl named Ellie. The child's father is still a part of her life but lives in a neighboring state and so only sees her every two months or so, though he gets her for six weeks every summer. Rob has been successful professionally. He has managed a number of local gyms and recently purchased his own. He has also made enough money to purchase two houses, both of which he has significantly remodeled, and one of which he now rents to tenants.

Becky is concerned about immediately moving into one of Rob's houses. Her separation from her boyfriend was only two years ago and it took some time for her and Ellie to settle back down. She is worried that moving again so soon could be awfully hard on her little girl. For his part Rob is worried about money. They make plenty between the two of them to support the family, and the extra income from renting out the house in which he is now living would more than balance out the shared rent on Becky's place, but he doesn't see the point in renting when he owns two houses of his own. Rob is also concerned that Becky never finished college because she got pregnant with Ellie. He'd prefer that they move into one of his houses and use the money they would have been spending on rent to have her go back to school at night and finish her degree. But every time Rob brings this up she gets very anxious. Becky was never very good at school, though she always managed to pass. She's worried about trying to go to school, work full time, and be a good mom. Plus she feels like she's not smart enough for Rob and his family. His parents are both professors and his brother is a priest. They always have deep conversations at family gatherings and she feels like she can't contribute. Her greatest fear is trying to go back to school and, instead of proving to herself that she can do it, proving to Rob and his family that she really isn't smart enough and therefore really doesn't belong with them, or with him.

Do you see how the cultural and structural concerns play out in a context like this? There are real and legitimate concerns about property, housing, work, and school but they are all bound up in bigger worries which involve things like communication, self-identity, and family culture. If Rob and Becky want to make the right structural decisions, they are going to first have to work out some of the cultural dynamics at play in their relationship so that they can decide together which values they want to protect and which ones they are comfortable letting go.

Rick and Katie are in a very different situation. They were close friends in high school, though they never dated, and largely went their separate ways after college. Rick became a software developer in Texas while Katie stayed in their hometown of Minneapolis to teach math at the high school they both attended. Rick married early and went through a divorce a couple of years later but has no children. Katie married about the same time and the marriage lasted for fifteen years and produced two children, but ended in an ugly divorce. They reconnected over Facebook, saw each other the first time again when Rick was home for Christmas, and made several trips back and forth before getting engaged. Rick is acquiring a lot in the merger: two rambunctious kids, Katie's elderly parents (with whom she presently lives), and a somewhat erratic ex-husband. Katie can't even figure out why he'd put himself through all of this. Rick, for his part, struggles to provide her with an adequate explanation other than that he loves her, feels she makes him a better man, and wants to be part of all of her life, even the parts she finds stressful, intimidating, or even embarrassing. They talk a lot about what they believe in, the values they hold, and how they want to live together as a family. They have a harder time agreeing on the practical side of things, principally where to live. Rick would prefer to raise the kids in Minnesota and certainly doesn't want to uproot Katie and her family to Texas, but is unsure that he can get a job with a comparable salary back home. Katie recognizes that if they stay in Minnesota, Rick will have to take a significant reduction in pay and radically change his lifestyle, and feels at a loss because he is giving up so much for her. The challenge for Rick and Katie is to translate their intercultural marriage merger into a practical one as well.

And so the challenge for you is to do the same. The culture of communication, finances, relating, family, life, love, sex, religion, and all the rest has to be tended to first in order that the structural adjustments which you make together well best serve the new entity which emerges: the couple and the family.

## Blending Family Cultures

Every marriage is, in a certain sense, a "mixed marriage," not in the sense that every marriage involves people from different religious traditions, but because the internal culture of each family is so different. In that sense the work of "blending" family cultures is essential to every marriage. This includes everything from negotiating holidays (either with or without the in-laws), to dividing up the labor of the house, to sorting out conflicts with the neighbors. While this is important for every marriage, the task of blending family cultures becomes especially important for families with children. Your kids aren't going to know, at least at first, that you open Christmas gifts on Christmas Eve because that's how Mommy's family did it, even though Dad always seems mildly annoyed. Children depend upon the grown-ups to hand them a culture which is meaningfully whole, whatever sources it might draw from. Grown-ups can always fall back on the family culture of their youth but part of your responsibility as parents is to help provide a family culture for your kids to grow up in.

Blending family cultures proves even more difficult when children come from previous relationships. Nationally speaking about 60% of all families have children from parents other than the ones primarily raising them at present. Parenting in blended families is not necessarily more difficult than parenting in general; one can have a traditionally-modeled family and have a very hard time raising the kids, and a multi-blended family where the task of childrearing seems to run quite smoothly, but there are necessarily some very distinct challenges.

First of all, depending upon the situation, children in blended families often find themselves belonging to at least two integral families at the same time. This is a difficult enough reality for an adult to negotiate, let alone for a child. This means that parents and stepparents will frequently have to use their best negotiating skills to address conflicts. These conflicts are inevitable, especially since differences in family culture and the inability to blend them often contributed to the failure of the first relationship. As a result they should be met head on and not simply compromised away. While compromise is a necessary and important negotiation tool, it is not the only one. For example, if establishing a consistent bedtime causes a constant conflict in the family, then simply negotiating on 9:30 as opposed to 9:00 or 10:00 may work in the short term, but long term both parents need to establish the values which are being prioritized which help one to arrive at an earlier or later bedtime. The important thing is to at least establish a clear and common plan together, even if it remains different from that of a previous partner.

Kids can work out that they have a different bedtime at Mom's house than at Dad's but it is much more difficult to figure out why sometimes bedtime at Dad's is the same time as at Mom's and sometimes it is not (like when Stepmom is around).

The key in all efforts at blending family cultures, whether with kids or without them, is to continually articulate the common plan which the two of you share as a couple as a way of fulfilling your vision as Christian spouses. If that vision remains paramount, and if that plan retains priority, then boundaries, house rules, and appropriate ways of relating will ultimately fall into place. Just making the vision and the plan your own, yours together, will make all the difference.

## Grace and Nature: Or, How Not to Lose Yourself

An absolutely bedrock principle of Catholic theology comes from St. Thomas Aquinas: "Grace does not destroy nature but perfects and fulfills it." This is important because in some Protestant theologies of grace it does precisely the opposite; grace so overwhelms our nature as to make it something different than it is. The point here is that the teaching has an important impact on both our theology of marriage and our lived experience of it. If grace destroys nature and replaces it with something else, then in marriage, which is the graced relationship in which one is drawn most closely into relationship with Christ, one would expect to lose one's self rather absolutely. If, on the other hand, grace perfects a nature which is already good, then the marriage will help you to become more yourself, to fulfill your potential more perfectly, and to become the person you were always meant to be—which is you but perfected in Christ.

What does this look like in concrete terms? Holidays are a good example. Major holidays are typically a major source of tension in the best of family situations, let alone in complex blended ones. If one partner comes from a large extended family that never passes up the opportunity to gather as a family and the other partner comes from a smaller, more intimate family tradition, then simply asserting one's own tradition can be intimidating to the one and isolating for the other. Developing your own family traditions, while still respecting that from which you both come, and integrating the existing family traditions is not only a particular way to compromise but can help you to retain a stronger sense of personal identity. One very practical way to accomplish this is to establish a new pattern at the outset, especially the first year you are married. Sometimes this means spending the whole holiday on your own, or maybe it means flipping around the times which you would normally spend with either side. But doing something significant and radical at the outset is probably the best way to establish your independence as a couple and to give yourselves the freedom to begin new traditions of your own.

Another important way is to grow is to frequently reaffirm in your partner those qualities about them which attracted you in the first place. If her independent streak and creativity is part of what drew you to her in the first place then don't let her lose her knack for jewelry-making or design work, even if it means giving up some space in the house for her to store her supplies. Likewise, if his introspection and reflective personality helps to inspire you then give him the time and space to study and affirm it in him so that he tends to that part of himself. The point of the marriage is that we become stewards, caretakers of one another's gifts and not simply of our own.

This is important because the tendency which most of us have will be to give until we've got no more, which will often result in losing the best of what we had to begin with.

**Recap**

- How is your family different from your parents' and grandparents'? How is this different from the family culture of your spouse's parents and grandparents?

- How does merging family cultures and acquiring new members affect the family culture which you have established? How can you be intentional about preserving the values which you hold most dear?

- What are three significant changes which you or your spouse are going to have to make to effectively build up the family culture which together you have agreed to work on?

- What does blending your own family with that your spouse actually look like? What fears do you have? What hopes for growth and change?

## Book II:  Where Are We Headed?

*"Do not let your hearts be troubled. You have faith in God; have faith also in me. In my Father's house there are many dwelling places. If there were not, would I have told you that I am going to prepare a place for you? And if I go and prepare a place for you, I will come back again and take you to myself, so that where I am you also may be. Where [I] am going you know the way." Thomas said to him, "Master, we do not know where you are going; how can we know the way?" Jesus said to him, "I am the way and the truth and the life. No one comes to the Father except through me." -Jn 14:1-6*

In Book I we looked closely at who you are as a couple. You explored your common values and ideals, and identified a common vision for your life together. In this second book we're going to get more practical. Having a common dream and establishing a common vision is only the first step in actually accomplishing them. In order to make things work you'll have to set up outcomes together, have common objectives that you can both meet and hold one another accountable to, and establish clear expectations for your relationship moving forward.

Budgets and chore schedules, mortgages and loan payments, holiday dinners and taking turns tending to sick kids might not sound like the most romantic thing in the world but in the long haul the spirituality of your marriage will be determined by how well you manage to do these things as a couple. A budget is a moral document, a family meeting is a spiritual exercise. You can accomplish the purpose of your marriage, you can have your dreams come true, and you can have something more besides. Budgets can be empowering when they're well done, and family meetings can be moments for real healing and growth— inasmuch as you both are growing more and more into the people you were always meant to be. That is, after all, the heart of the matter, the mission of your marriage from beginning to end.

# CHAPTER 4:
# Eye on the Prize:
# Setting Objectives and Working to Achieve Them

Hopefully by now you see the value of a "We" as opposed to a "me" approach in thinking about and living your marriage. You are now a part of a new community, even if that community only consists of two people, and so the decisions you make, prospects you consider, and consequences you endure will not only be your own but your spouse's also. The benefits of belonging to such a community far outweigh the deficits but one of the most important is this: having established a vision for yourselves, identified core values, and produced powerful common symbols, you now know what you stand for—together. You no longer have to make decisions based upon a kind of cost-benefit analysis of what you like vs. what you can afford. Your priorities ought to have changed. The questions you now ask should center around "us" and "our objectives" as opposed to "me" and "my wants." This is part of how marriage serves to make you and your spouse into better people.

This doesn't happen automatically, though. You both have to be intentional about working to achieve the common dream. But ideals can be overwhelming, and because they are only attained in the long haul they can seem, on a day-to-day basis, elusive. One of the most important things you do in your relationship, then, will be to periodically set clear, obtainable, and measurable objectives with and for each other which will help you together to win the prize which you both seek.

## Chapter Objectives
- Identify ways to employ a common vision without losing yourself in the process.
- Brainstorm with your partner at least five of the objective dimensions categories provided in the chapter.
- Establish three objectives to attain in the next six months.

## Setting Objectives

Everyone needs an objective to work for, it's basic to the human spirit. Hopefully in putting together your Vision Statement you two have come to something of an understanding of what you are for together. The question now is just how to get there.

Setting objectives is the first step to attaining your dream. You need to return to that ideal state of your relationship which helped you to write your Vision Statement. What was the condition of the possibility for the things which you proposed; in other words, what things will be necessary to help you accomplish your dreams, to realize your vision? What kind of financial independence do you need? What kind of work will you need to be doing? How does advancement at work play into your overall career plans? How do children fit into the plan of your marriage? What will you do with aging parents and/or other sick relatives? What are your contingency plans in case of catastrophic disaster or accidents? You need to consider all of these things as you move forward to set up your objectives.

Feel free to dream big but when you sit down to articulate these objectives make them as specific and clear as you can. "We want to be reasonably well-off" is a noble sentiment but a poorly written objective. How would you ever know if you accomplished it? "We want our collective income to exceed $70,000 per year by the time we are 40." That's short, measureable, clear, pithy, and has a time limit. "We both want to obtain a master's degree in our respective fields within five years of marriage." This is a good objective but it might need broken down a bit. You might say, "Well, she needs an MBA and I need an M.Ed. Her MBA will undoubtedly make her more money so she should get hers first to help pay for my education." Then, as you take care of the children more often so that she can take classes and study, you become invested in her degree. By the time you get to her graduation, which is also the halfway point to your graduation, you have both become seriously invested in one another's degrees. This is why having clear ultimate objectives is so important.

# Writing Relationship Objectives

While writing the Vision Statement was initially a solitary exercise which we eventually brought together, setting common objectives is generally an exercise best done together. Individual objectives will certainly still be a part of your life, and part of what you share together in your marriage will be the hard work of attaining those objectives, but they should always be in tandem with and in a certain sense subservient to the common objectives of the relationship. Writing objectives alone often gets us into trouble because it allows us to focus too exclusively on ourselves and slip back more easily into "me-speak," as opposed to "we-speak."

Decide at the outset what dimension of your relationship you want to explore together. Are the objectives you're going to explore today related to your family life? Are they more concerned with your financial situation? Are you exploring individual career paths and the effects which they may or may not have on your life together as a couple and/or a family?

What we're really talking about here is strategic planning for the marriage. Organizations of all types have practiced strategic planning for decades. Here's an acronym that they often use to ensure they set a clear objective as part of the planning process: Be S.M.A.R.T.

Objectives should be:

**SPECIFIC** – Objectives need to be concrete and clear. It's better to have more objectives which are easily distinguishable from one another than vague statements which you may never be able to tell have been accomplished.

**MEASURABLE** – The objectives themselves are part of how you mark progress towards the vision. Thus the objectives themselves need to be mark-able; that is, it should be clear whether progress is being made and when the objective has been reached.

**ACHIEVABLE** – The objectives are tools to help you accomplish your common vision. If you want to actually be able to accomplish the vision you have set out for yourselves then the objectives along the way need to be reasonably attainable.

**RELEVANT** – Objectives need to be the bridge between where your relationship is really today and where you'd really like for it to be someday. They should not only be identifiable and attainable and measurable things which can be done together but should actually further your vision together.

**TIME-BOUND** – Specific dates need to be attached to specific objectives to ensure that they actually are met. Timelines help to keep us all on track, make sure that we know when we're achieving our objectives and when we're not, and can also help us to clarify the nature of the vision.

## Multi-dimensional Categories

You will probably find it helpful to brainstorm your objectives by category which will help you to realize all of the many ways in which particular objectives are related to one another. Obviously financial objectives and your ability to meet them will have a direct bearing on your educational objectives and leisure plans. Career objectives can impact heavily whether or not you choose to buy or rent, stay in one place or move around, and how much you choose to invest in personal relationships in a particular space. And, most importantly, your spiritual objectives should, in a certain sense, be directing and coordinating your other concerns.

Here are some typical categories that cover a broad range of your activities as a couple and a family. Consider these as you prepare to develop your set of S.M.A.R.T. objectives for each category that defines your life together.

**Family** – Setting clear objectives for family life is important from the start. The question of the number and spacing of children figures in prominently here but so do things like managing relationships with in-laws, contact (or lack thereof) with particular parts of the family, care of sick or elderly parents and relatives, and perhaps even some close friendships outside of the family proper. But these decisions have a serious bearing on a host of other concerns in your life. Family planning depends in large measure on the character of your intimate life together. Managing relationships has everything to do with how you handle your free time. And all of these bear directly upon your financial life.

**Financial** – How much money do each of you make now? What are your respective earning potentials ultimately? Do one or both of you want to continue your careers or does one of you want to stay home? What does retirement look like for you? How much do you need to start saving now in order to be able to afford a meaningful retirement later? Are your kids going to go to Catholic schools, public schools, or will you homeschool? How much money do you need to ensure appropriate leisure for each member of the family? Do you have a rainy day fund? How much money is in it? What would you do tomorrow if one of you suffered a catastrophic injury or debilitating illness?

**Health and Well-Being** – Are you both fitness buffs? Do you simply want to avoid an early heart attack? Or are you both content with being couch potatoes? Probably that last one won't help either of you attain your personal or collective dreams but what are reasonable expectations of health and wellness for the both of you? How do you plan on being an example of healthy living for you kids? How do you handle injury and disease? What provision have you made for each other's psychological health? How would you support one another in a period of depression, anger, or need? How do you both feel about psychotherapy? If it became necessary would you be willing to engage in counseling, not only for your own sake but also for the sake of your spouse? How will you organize your time so that you are sufficiently present to each other, and together present to others as well?

**Intimacy** – Intimacy is far more than just sex, although in a healthy Christian marriage sex is an essential component of the relationship. How will you make your own intimate and sexual desires known? What agreed upon ways of dealing with each other's need for intimacy will you respond to? How will you communicate an inability to answer a need at a particular point without expressing rejection to your spouse? How will you work to be the right person for your spouse in your intimate relations? How will you communicate your needs to your spouse to help make them a better person?

**Recreation** – Relaxing, recharging, and rejuvenating ourselves helps us literally to re-create ourselves and our world. How will you regularly recreate, both alone and together? Will you take nightly walks together or will you run in the morning? Will you travel together every summer or donate a week to Habitat for Humanity locally? Trips to the ski lodge each winter will obviously impact your financial decisions but so will regular campouts in the summer, albeit in very different ways. What about daily hobbies and supplies? How does this affect your community involvement?

**Relationships** – No marriage is for the couple alone. You will need to have and sustain outside relationships to remain healthy together. The question is which relationships, and what should they look like? Are you comfortable with your spouse having friends of the opposite sex with whom they spend time alone? What are your natural forums for friendship: work, school, church, the public library? How do these relationships bear on your own marital relationship and your relationship to your kids and the rest of your family?

**Career** – First, it should be established that, for both of you, your marriage is your primary career. Anything else you or your spouse do is a "second" career and should be viewed through the perspective of your vision and what is best for your family as a whole. How important is an outside career to either of you? If one or the other is forced to quit a job, how will that decision be made? What kinds of moves, adjustments, shifts, and the like are you willing to make as a couple and what concessions to work are absolutely off the table? What sort of values will you use to make decisions about work and family life?

**Education** – Every Christian has a serious obligation to develop her intellect to the best of her ability according to her station in life. What space will you leave open in your marriage for ongoing education, both formal and informal? What sorts of hobbies, practices, and opportunities will help you to grow intellectually, both individually and as a couple? How can improving your intellectual life serve to better inform your practice of the Faith?

**Religion and Spirituality** – A robust spirituality of married life needs to be at the foundation of each of these categories. How will you continue to grow in your common vision of marriage and family life? What is reasonable to expect from your spouse spiritually and what spiritual needs will have to be fulfilled individually? How do your respective spiritualties differ? How are they the same? How can you challenge one another to grow spiritually? What are potential points of conflict or discord in your spiritual life?

We often think of religious as being the ones who take a vow of poverty but we married Christians are called to a kind of poverty too. Monks and nuns agree to have nothing as their own, to "hold all things in common." In Christian marriage you too will hold all things in common, and not only your bank accounts. Your religious and spiritual struggles will impact your spouse's personal and emotional objectives. Your spouse's educational objectives will impact your financial situation. Your collective desire for leisure will dramatically affect both how much you work and how you spend your free time. The key, as with everything, is clear communication from the start.

## The Importance of Clear Milestones

Just as specific objectives are important, so are clear milestones. You need to know not only when you've reached your objectives but also when you're reasonably close to doing so. Life can easily become drudgery if all you do is look forward to what will be without reference to what is right now.

As you lay out your end objectives and determine a reasonable timeline, consider ways in which you can mark intermediate accomplishments as you go along. So, for instance, while paying off the mortgage and having a mortgage-burning party is a worthwhile objective, most people aren't going to be able to do that for quite a number of years. But if you purchase a bottle of wine every $5,000 in mortgage reduction, then you can reasonably celebrate your thrift while at the same time not seriously diminishing your chances of accomplishing your end objectives.

A major portion of what you and your spouse will be doing with each other throughout all of this is helping one another to cultivate virtue. Particular good habits are going to be important for accomplishing particular objectives.

For instance, patience and perseverance will be important for completing a master's degree; bravery will be required to try and change career fields; temperance will be necessary in order to lose weight. The real virtue which you will both be developing in the midst of all of this, however, is prudence. Prudence is the gambler's virtue: it's knowing when to hold and when to fold, and having the courage to do it. Cultivating prudence in the particular aspects of your married life will serve as the basis for the next several chapters.

## Recap

- Marriage is about a "We" not a "me"
- If you want to achieve your objectives as a couple set them together
- Individual objectives are still important but they need to be integrated into the wider vision of the couple and the family
- Smaller, time-bound objectives help us to work towards our vision
- Celebrating little victories along the way together is the key to successfully attaining your common objectives

# CHAPTER 5:
## Funding the Vision:
## Financial Transparency and Personal Serenity

*"A budget is more than a series of facts and figures...It is a moral document, revealing our deepest values and spiritual commitments..."* — *Cardinal Timothy Dolan, Archbishop of New York*

As the quote above underscores: budgets matter. It matters where we get our money. And most of all, it matters how we decide to spend our money. Jesus says, "Where your treasure is, there your heart will be also" (Mt 6:21). In other words, if you want to see what you really value, look at how you spend your money and utilize your other resources. If we have a Vision as couples, and as families, then the way we use our resources should reflect the values most central to our Vision.

## Chapter Objectives
- Understand why financial concerns are such a struggle even in healthy marriages, and why conversations about money tend to cause so much anxiety.
- Identify at least three financial myths.
- Explain the importance of articulating clearly the overall values which guide your financial philosophy.

## You Can't See Me...

We've all played this game with a little one before, right? As the child begins to understand how Peek-a-Boo works she'll cover up her own eyes and say, "You can't see me," and squeal with delight. She's realized that when she covers her eyes she can't see you and presumes that if she can't see you that you can't see her. Of course, she is mistaken; so are the millions of couples who choose to simply ignore the importance of finances in their life together. Your Vision has to be funded some way or another and if your resources (which are not limited to money) fail then your marriage will flounder.

Many couples avoid or even refuse to engage in the financial conversation. This is often due to a perceived difference in financial philosophies early on in the relationship. Whether it's because she is thrifty and he's a spender, or he's an accountant and so she presumes that he should run the family finances, refusing to share equally in the financial responsibility of the household can result in major hurdles for your relationship. One of you is probably better suited to manage the household finances than the other but you need to be clear early on about attitudes, expectations, and values so that there's no confusion and hurt feelings later. In that respect, your financial life isn't so different than most of the rest of your marriage. In the end, it's all about communicating clear expectations and values with regard to family finances.

Therefore this chapter is not about the best investments, most lucrative retirement plans, or the best sort of life insurance policy to purchase to protect your family. This is about funding the Vision, the charge which you and your spouse have been given by Christ and His Church, and the particular way in which you will bring that Vision to life in your own marriage and family life. In order to do that you need to be sure that the resources, both financial and otherwise, are there to back the Vision itself, as well as to articulate the attitudes which you each have and the values which you will come to share, which should determine how you earn, manage, and spend your money.

## To Thine Own Self Be True

For most of us, our attitudes toward money, how it is spent, and the role it should play in our overall life are learned in childhood. Usually our spending habits, investment practices, and use of resources are a product of our family of origin. Sometimes if our family's financial practices were either excessively extravagant or stiflingly severe then our own habits were established as a kind of rejection of what we grew up with. In either case, before you can engage the tough financial questions which you will need to face with your partner, you need to first be clear about what your own fiscal practices have been and are, and what you'd like to see for your life together.

What is your relationship to money? Is it a means to an end, an end in itself, or is it something more? Do you fear spending money, hoarding every cent and spending it only when absolutely necessary? Or do you spend money freely and often find yourself living paycheck-to-paycheck or relying on large credit card balances? What is your debt history and how has it affected your current spending practices? Are you coming into this relationship with significant student loans? Do you have any personal, non-educational debt? If so, where did this come from and how do you mean to pay it off? What is your own attitude towards debt? How does it affect you personally, morally, and spiritually? How do you spend your disposable income? What would you be comfortable with your partner spending? Do you have any investments? Have you started saving for your retirement? Is it important that one of you stay home with the kids? Do you think one partner should necessarily make significantly more of the household income than the other? What sort of rainy-day fund or emergency plan do you maintain? Where do you go when you need financial help and advice? What would you do if you had to declare bankruptcy?

These and other questions should get you thinking. No one of them should be understood as definitive of your whole financial philosophy but, taken together, they should give you a pretty clear sense of your relationship to money.

## Family Financial Myths

Once you have arrived at a realistic understanding of your own relationship to money you will be ready to engage in the conversation together. It's important to do some of that early reflection on your own so that you don't find yourself too influenced by your partner. The tendency here may be that one of you will give in to the other, but you must not do that. Even if one of you has significantly better financial skills than the other you must talk about these things together. It's the only way to ever really get both of you on the same page and avoid the deep resentments that can arise later from years of feeling out of financial control of one's life.

Almost invariably a problem which one or both of you will encounter in these early conversations together are what we call "Family Financial Myths." Because most of us learn about personal financing from our parents and families of origin a whole host of attitudes, perceptions, and practices will seemingly be unquestioned when it comes to money. If your spouse grew up in a family where money was always tight and where it was a struggle just to get by, then money and conversations about money may cause a great deal of anxiety. If your spouse came from a lot of money then they may be simply unaware of the necessity of things like budgets or they might be excessively concerned with things like investments. Be attentive to the anxiety, both your own and your spouse's, and take time to acknowledge it so that a strong emotional response doesn't dominate or determine your own attitude toward money.

Past financial failures need not determine the future either. As with any other kind of failure we can tend to presume that because it has happened once it will happen again. We can play the same "broken record" over and over again in our heads. "I'm not good with money," or "You can't balance a checkbook." None of these things are true but, in order to ensure that they don't come true, three things need to happen at the outset. First, you need to take full responsibility for whatever failure was reasonably yours. If you were in college and simply didn't know how to properly use a credit card and so ran up a bunch of debt, then take responsibility for it. If, on the other hand, one of your parents died or became seriously ill, or your personal finances were wrapped up somehow in a family business, or your identity was stolen, then, while you may have some small measure of responsibility, you clearly can't blame yourself in the same way. Don't take responsibility for things that aren't your responsibility. Nobody else's financial mistakes are your own; not your parents', not your family's, not your friends', not even a former spouse's. Next, commit to doing things differently. Study up on whatever went wrong, educate yourself better about finances in general, and, most importantly, tune out those voices who only warn of doom, disaster, and failure. Just because something was one way a long time ago doesn't mean it has to be that way again. Finally, use the resources at your disposal. If you don't understand something, even if it seems basic and you feel like you should already know it, ask your spouse. If your spouse asks you something and you don't know the answer then between the two of you one of you probably knows someone else who knows the answer. If not, find it; use the Internet, the local library, or, if you need to, hire a professional. If the two of you both are feeling significantly deficient in financial matters then think about attending a workshop or taking a class together at your parish or the local community college. Whatever you do, realize that your future together is determined by the two of you and God; nobody else's past, habits, or ways of doing things can control you.

## Dealing with Differences

That being said, how can you deal with the genuine differences in financial philosophy that may arise, especially if you come from two very different family, social, and economic perspectives? Use the skills you've been developing all along the way to facilitate, manage, and negotiate conflict. Don't presume at the outset that there has to be a winner and a loser. Don't set out to persuade but to understand. Don't decide that you can simply change the person over time by force of will, any change requires an open and honest exchange. Don't decide simply, "I'll take care of this" or, conversely, "I'll just let you handle it." Do name your feelings, even your feelings about your partner's feelings. Do affirm your partner in those places where you can honestly affirm them and assure them that they are not bound by their financial past (even if they are bound to it, say, by way of debt). Do give substantive reasons for your own position. Do welcome authentic compromise. Do be willing to let this feature of the relationship, as with the others, grow over time.

None of this is to say that conflicts over money aren't real or ought to be glossed over. On the contrary, if you have fundamentally different financial philosophies from the outset then you both have to commit to a certain level of change if you even hope for the relationship to have a chance. This is why framing the financial question in moral and spiritual terms is so important. "How much money should go into savings every month?" is not the right question to start with. Rather, you should start by reflecting on the values which you have already established that you share. What kind of lifestyle do you hope to maintain? What are your authentic monetary needs? What are your genuine wants? What role should charity play in your financial life together? What causes are really important to you both? What expectations do you both have about leisure/recreation? Do you think your partner's expectations are reasonable? Why or why not?

While it is important, especially early on, to not "harp" on the issue of money all of the time, if even broaching these issues together or initiating the financial conversation seems to be causing lots of undue stress then it may be that some more serious counseling is needed. This might be financial counseling, it might be psychological counseling, or it might be a combination of both. Our attitudes about money come from various sources: home and family life, education, our own economic background, the media, our peers, society in general, and even religion. This is why it is so important to be clear about the core values of the relationship before approaching the money question. The way we spend our money should reflect our deeper values, not the other way around. Financial serenity is possible but it may not be easy to achieve... but then again nothing worthwhile ever is.

## Money, The Root of All Evil?

One way in which the Christian tradition in particular has contributed to a certain amount of financial anxiety is that the Church's position on money seems somewhat ambivalent at times. Parish priests are often forced to ask for money a lot because Catholics tend not to tithe (donate) well. At the same time, Catholic religious (monks, friars, nuns, sisters, etc.) take a vow of poverty and refuse to own personal property. Much of the Church's work is taken up in offering care for the poor and disadvantaged and we even preach a "preferential option for the poor." Combine that with a quote rolling around somewhere in the back of most people's heads that the Bible says somewhere, "Money is the root of all evil,' and you've got a perfect storm.

The quote is, of course, inaccurate. The citation is actually from 1 Timothy 6:10 and what it says is: "The **love** of money is the root of all evil." HUGE DIFFERENCE. Money is a morally neutral means of economic exchange but a disordered desire for money, or other assets, is "the root of all evil" because the desire is itself disordered. It confuses the means for the end, the tools to get there with the prize itself.

This concern may show up most with dual income couples since it's easy for a lot of couples today, especially young couples, to fall into the trap of "needing" both incomes. It may well be that given your financial state you actually do need two incomes, especially given today's economy, but the mistake which couples often make is deciding in the abstract about a particular lifestyle they want to maintain, recognizing that both partners will have to work full time in order to maintain it, and then resenting work because they have to spend so much time apart in order to earn the money to maintain the lifestyle which they mean to enjoy together. Do you see the financial paradox that can prevent financial serenity? This can happen to couples from every sort of economic background but it's especially important to consider when children come along. In the cost-benefit analysis of your life, does paying for full time day care really pay off?

The point is that more money doesn't always result in more happiness. In fact, very often, it results in less. The important thing is that money is a means to an end. Love your spouse. Love your kids. Love your life together. Be grateful for what you have. Use your money to best provide for your family. But don't love your money, or you just might wind up loving it more than your family.

## The Price of Freedom

There's an old saying from the Great Depression, "There ain't no shame in being poor; it's just damned inconvenient." What money ultimately buys us is freedom from certain burdens and worries. This is the reason that so many anxieties attach themselves to money: what they represent is the difference between poverty and plenty. Money, or lack thereof, reminds us that poverty leads to a kind of slavery and winds up inhibiting our actions. Nobody wants to be enslaved to poverty and so it's important to at least have the financial resources to function.

Which is not to say that this needs to look the same for everybody. It might be argued that this very attitude towards money, resources, and financial freedom is painfully middle-class but it need not necessarily be so. The question of freedom is at the heart of the Church's teaching on poverty. The "preferential option for the poor" is not about Jesus loving poor people more than rich ones; after all, He dined at the houses of the scribes and Pharisees as well as the poor. What it's about is recognizing that impoverishment inhibits people's freedoms and prevents them from making their own decisions and caring for themselves, whether that impoverishment is material or spiritual.

It turns out that you really don't need the latest electronics, a fancy vacation, or even brand name clothes to be happy. You just need to have access to those things which authentically fulfill your needs, and the freedom to engage those things which will make you a better person.

Christians are called to "poverty," that is, to simplicity of life, because of the example of Jesus Himself. That's why, whether you're a religious or a married layman, the goal of poverty is the same:

> Poverty proclaims that God is man's only real treasure. When poverty is lived according to the example of Christ who, "though he was rich... became poor" (2 Cor 8:9), it becomes an expression of that total gift of self which the three Divine Persons make to one another (JP II, *Vita Consecrata*, 21).

In our lives together we always point to something more, something deeper, whether we mean to or not. This is why the fiscal and financial decisions you make as a couple not only determine whether or not you can accomplish your Vision as a couple but also the way in which you are contributing, as a couple, as families, and as individuals, to the mission of the Church herself.

## Recap

- Do financial conversations cause you or your partner anxiety? If so, why do you think this is the case? Does this match your partner's impression of the situation or not?
- What are the financial myths prevalent in your own family? What about your partner's? How can you help each other to overcome the anxiety attached to these myths?
- What are the values which you two will use to guide your overall financial philosophy? How will these help you to accomplish your common mission and so attain the common vision you laid out in the first chapter?

# CHAPTER 6:
## Job Descriptions for Couples:
## The Importance of Expectations

*"Oh, yeah, life goes on, long after the thrill of livin' is gone."*
*– John Mellencamp*

Everyone knows that young couples newly in love are on a kind of emotional "high." Part of the reason most people advise against short engagements these days is because once the "high" has worn off you can suffer from a kind of "infatuation hangover" and the marriage can wind up doomed almost before it has a chance to really blossom. At the same time, you need to find ways to continue to sustain positive feelings towards you partner. Whether we like to admit it or not (and most guys will not) our feelings and emotions are one of our primary motivators. It's certainly possible to keep a marriage together long after all emotional connection has been lost but it's a whole lot easier to do if you can keep the connection going. That isn't to say that every day should feel like your wedding day; instead, it's about training your more fickle emotions to respond to the right sort of things and so sustain the love which together you have forged.

## Chapter Objectives

- Explain the importance of clear expectations in a relationship.
- Identify basic skill sets for both you and your partner.
- Discuss ways in which the work of the relationship can be fairly divided.
- Identify the essential components of a job description.
- Come up with meaningful job descriptions for both you and your partner which include reasonable and clear expectations.
- Reflect upon the ongoing importance of your marriage vows in your relationship.

## Dishes, Tasks, and Daily Chores

The major day-to-day task of your relationship is to protect, develop, and sustain the love and romance in your marriage. By minimizing those things which typically erode positive feeling towards your partner and your life together—stress, resentment over household tasks, family disagreements or rifts, financial burdens, and all the rest—you can focus better on the ideals and vision which you have developed to give your marriage purpose and to enjoy it along the way. The bottom line is that we cannot possibly meet expectations if we do not know what is expected of us in the first place.

One of the most important things to ensure success in any organization, be it a business, a church, a school, or even a marriage, is to have a clear, reasonable, and attainable job descriptions for everyone involved. Job descriptions tell you what is expected of you in performing your job, as well as providing role clarity. In a marriage, both partners are equal contributors and the way in which you perform the tasks assigned to you makes up your contribution.

In responsible businesses, every employee has a job description. Some job descriptions are highly formalized and extremely specific. Others amount to a general list of tasks and responsibilities. If a company didn't give an employee a job description it wouldn't run very efficiently and might ultimately break down. The same can happen in a marriage.

You may have never considered applying such a common sense business principle to your marriage but now is the time to do it. You need job descriptions that lay out clearly what each of you will do daily to help sustain your marriage. Still not convinced? Alright, think of it this way: Do you really think that your spouse has a very clear understanding of what you expect of him all of the time? Do you think she really knows what it is that you're doing in that home office all day?

If you've ever had any kind of a conflict over expectations for who is to complete what daily tasks, then a Relationship Job Description is the tool for you. What the job description does is make sure that everyone is on the same page (literally) so that the hard work of being a couple and a family can be shared by all, according to their abilities and preferences.

Disagreements over chores is one of the most common sources of marital conflicts. That's why it is so important to develop good job descriptions and clear expectations from the beginning, to safeguard your relationship, improve your emotional state relative to your marriage, and protect the values which you both hold most dear.

## Clarity Is Key

Conflicts in relationship often stem from the same root problem: unfulfilled expectations. Think about how often you've heard this at work:

- You should've known better; you've been with the company for years!
- Nobody else had trouble understanding what to do!
- You were at the meeting just like everybody else! Why didn't you get the message?

Now compare these to the number of times you've heard this kind of thing at home:

- You know that I hate it when you...
- My (Mom/Dad/Old Boyfriend) never had trouble figuring this out.
- We talked about this last week. Don't you even listen to me anymore?

There's a kind of a golden rule for relationships: If you habitually fail to meet your partner's expectations, don't expect them to meet yours either.

This is why role clarity is so important. In an orchestra, a flute player knows that she will not be playing the kettle drum. Likewise, a place-kicker knows that he won't be starting at quarterback in the second half. In a marriage, both spouses will need to work towards common objectives by matching the tasks to be performed with the competencies, interests, and availability of each spouse. At the same time, the phrase "It's not my job" simply has no place on the tongue of a dedicated spouse.

In the recent past—think especially of your grandparents' generation here—household tasks were largely based on gender-specific job descriptions which clearly distinguished "men's work" from "women's work." This was often done without respect to competencies; that is, whether or not the spouse assigned the task was actually able to perform it well. It may have made some sense in times past, especially in those places where "work" was synonymous with hard manual labor, that men do the "heavy lifting." Even then, however, women played an equally important role in performing the manual tasks of running the household.

A number of things have changed that picture: modern conveniences, labor-saving appliances, wider availability of goods which were once only made at home, migration patterns to the cities and away from the country, and a general re-evaluation of gender roles in society.

The Church has a great interest in this reevaluation. This is because, contrary to popular mythology, the Catholic Church has more often been an agent of change with regard to women's rights than an obstacle to them. The Church acknowledges, respects, and demands the legal equality of men and women. At the same time, it recognizes that men and women are different and that this difference is not simply culturally conditioned.

"Dad" is not simply the word for "male-mom" and neither is "Mom" the word for "female-dad." Moms and dads are different, as are brothers and sisters, and husbands and wives, and this difference is not simply in terms of biology or chemistry—it touches on the very dignity of the human person. Further, this difference is a *good* thing. Man and woman are not polar opposites at odds with one another but they complement each other and, together, reveal what it means to be fully human. The mistake of much modern gender revision is to equate equality with sameness which, in the realm of human sexuality, necessarily means to separate sex from procreation, its highest purpose.

All that being said, one clear improvement in gender fairness are laws which protect women's rights in the workplace. Insisting that only women make the coffee or men move the furniture would open up an employer for a gender discrimination lawsuit, and rightly so. At the same time, many of us engage in this same sort of "illegal" activity at home. Studies continually reveal that most working women believe that the household work should be shared with their spouses. Men tend to agree on the surveys but not in practice. Instead, women continue to do the bulk of the work associated with homemaking and childrearing, and this is a serious problem. By and large, men simply do not hold up their end of the bargain.

The core competencies of any marriage include skills in life management, communication, negotiations and problem solving, sound mental and physical health, child rearing, romance, and intimacy—yes, being romantic and intimate are skills that can be learned and enhanced. The process of discerning and developing competencies, of respecting issues which your spouse is still working through, and challenging them to grow even more is at the heart of a good job description and clear expectations.

If love were simply a business, based upon sound business principles, the relationship would need to be driven by competency-based job descriptions regardless of gender. However, given the nature of a sacramental marriage, a marriage intended not only to permit the couple to live in harmony but to help each member thrive and grow closer to God through the other, then something more must be at the heart of how we determine who performs which tasks. Surely the man may cook and the woman may garden, provided that the man *can* cook and the woman has a green thumb.

But what if the man is an excellent cook but hates to do it or the woman grew up on a farm but moved to the city for a reason? Couples should not only help to determine each other's competencies but also their passions. If he loves to cook, if he takes delight in feeding you, your children, and your friends, then most of the time he probably should. And if she loves to work with her hands and can keep up with the house and the lawn and the cars then she should do so. Marriage is not only about doing what you want to (and certainly we all have to do things that we don't particularly want to do in life) but we should make sure that the things we ask each other to do are actually good for the other. The key is not only to match the person most qualified for the job, though that's important, but also to match the person with their passion. The best businesses know this too and, by doing so, get the highest quality of work out of their employees.

Children are another key factor in determining and fulfilling job descriptions. How you live your marriage will be the most important model and example for your kids in their own relationships and family life. You model your key values and articulate an implicit philosophy of life to your kids by the tasks you choose and how you perform them. What kind of message do you send about women to your son when he sees you sitting on the couch watching TV while his mom does the dishes and cleans the house (even though you both work full time jobs outside of the house)? Do you even believe in this image of marriage and family? Is this the happy sort of life you described together in your Vision Statement for you, your spouse, and your children?

Let's put it differently: How do you think your spouse will feel after years of doing all of the tasks that she loathes and you refuse to share? Do you think she'll be inclined to feel charitable towards you (the whole purpose of your marriage, after all) if you never lift a finger to help with the most unpleasant or mundane of chores? Relationships, like everything else, are based on cause and effect. What you get is a direct result of, and will be in proportion to, what you give (or fail to give).

Think back to your experience either at work or in school. Surely you can remember a time when a team member wasn't pulling his or her weight. How did you feel when someone you had the right to expect something out of failed to do his fair share? How did you react? Whether you said so or not, you were surely angry and resentful. Now think about your spouse's feelings when she is forced to do more than her due and you sit around and wonder why "She's lost that lovin' feeling!" If you and your spouse do not mutually determine equitable job descriptions and support one another in your efforts to fulfill them, then you will have conflict. The only question is whether or not the damage will be reparable by the time the conflict overwhelms you.

## Bringing Your Work Home

It may help to complete the following activity by first looking at your own job description from your place of work (if you have one). First, it may reference larger responsibilities, such as overseeing marketing, sales, operations, training, etc. Then it probably focuses on specific tasks, such as implementing an inventory automation system, providing training programs, managing the budget, producing a profit-and-loss statement for the department, or overseeing the development of online content for the website. Basically, it lays out your larger responsibilities in the organization as a whole and then the specific tasks which you are to perform to make your job more successful.

The same principles should govern your own relationship. First you need to refer to your Vision Statement, then you need to decide together who will be doing the larger tasks by category: maintaining the household, taking care of the kids, caring for ailing parents, financial planning, etc. After this you can move onto more specific tasks such as figuring out who does what around the house and outside of it.

## Sample Summary Job Descriptions

### For a part-time working wife and mom
General:
- My overall responsibility is being the primary caretaker of our children, a good partner to my husband, and coordinating household tasks which have to do with the kitchen and bathrooms.

- Additionally I will work 18-25 hours a week to cover the tuition costs for preschool and additional activities for the kids while achieving intellectual stimulation and career growth.


### For a full-time working husband and dad

General:

- My overall responsibility is to work to bring in most of the income, to cover expenses and investment/retirement plans, and achieve intellectual stimulation and career growth.
- Regular daily presence to be a good father to our children and a helpful partner to my wife.

## Sources for your marital job description

Businesses rely upon a variety of sources for writing job descriptions: corporate standards and benchmarks, projections, the experience of previous employees and supervisors, and even input from the potential employees themselves. Marriages aren't so different. Whether you have already developed a job description for your marriage or not, you have internalized many of your expectations based upon your experience of other people's marriages, especially your own parents' marriage.

Draw upon these resources as richly as you can but be discerning, for not all marriages are the same, and even some very good marriages can have a different recipe for success than is appropriate for the two of you.

It probably shouldn't surprise us that the Church herself offers us some resources that pertain precisely to a Christian view of marriage. Since the marriage is itself bound up with the consent which you offer to each other, the wedding vows themselves might be a helpful place to start.

At the wedding, both parties say:

> I, (name), take you, (name), to be my wife (husband). I promise to be true to you in good times and in bad, in sickness and in

health. I will love you and honor you all the days of my life. (*Rite of Marriage*, 25.)

So, at least in principle, the basic job description of the spouses is to live a life of self-donation to the other, no matter what, until death. That is at once both a pretty tall and a pretty vague work order.

For something slightly more descriptive we might turn to the *Catechism*. It says, among other things:

> The matrimonial covenant, by which a man and a woman establish between themselves a partnership of the whole of life, is by its nature ordered toward the good of the spouses and the procreation and education of offspring; this covenant between baptized persons has been raised by Christ the Lord to the dignity of a sacrament (*Catholic Church* 1601).

Finally, the *Catechism* lays out what is specifically Christian about Christian marriage.

> Conjugal love involves a totality, in which all the elements of the person enter—appeal of the body and instinct, power of feeling and affectivity, aspiration of the spirit and of will. It aims at a deeply personal unity, a unity that, beyond union in one flesh, leads to forming one heart and soul; it demands indissolubility and faithfulness in definitive mutual giving; and it is open to fertility. In a word it is a question of the normal characteristics of all natural conjugal love but with a new significance which not only purifies and strengthens them but raises them to the extent of making them the expression of specifically Christian values (*Catholic Church* 1643).

The Church is simply echoing her Founder:

> "For this reason a man shall leave his father and mother [and be joined to his wife], and the two shall become one flesh." So

they are no longer two but one flesh. Therefore what God has joined together, no human being must separate (Mk 10:7-9).

All of this is just to say that the job description for a marriage in the Church should look different from that of other people precisely because the individual life of a Christian should be different from other people: there is a higher calling and more being asked of us. It's important, then, that as you arrive at a division of labor and sense of purpose that, if you intend to do so as Christians, you make sure you know what makes your marriage Christian.

## Your Marital Job Description

Before you begin, think of your relationship as an organization that places both you and your spouse in executive roles—maybe Chairman and President, or co-CEOs, or co-Presidents, or just plain old partners. The title you pick is not nearly as important as the concept that you are both equally invested and so equally share in responsibility and authority.

Now, take a look at your relationship objectives from Chapter 4 and use that as a framework to begin to list all of the various tasks and responsibilities which will need to be taken care of if you and your household are to function.

You can write your job descriptions separately or together. One helpful exercise can be to work solo when you first start to write the job descriptions then share them with your partner. When you see the disparity between your two sets of descriptions, use those as talking points to work out mutually agreeable descriptions together. Choose whichever way works for you as a couple. You probably are growing in your understanding of the dynamics which tend to dominate in your relationship from the previous exercises.

Next write an overview of what role(s) you've agreed upon and have your partner do the same. This will serve as the basis for the specific responsibilities section yet to come. Now you are ready to engage the concrete realities of your life together. You have moved beyond the conceptual "big picture" issues, which can be difficult to determine and combine on their own, and are now in the thick of the concrete issues that affect you on a daily basis.

Below is an Example Monthly Planning Worksheet which should give you an idea of how to record not only what things have to be done to keep the household going but also the time and money involved (especially important if you are not/have not been the one doing this task), as well as the role of that particular task in your overall relationship. Please note that these tasks will also serve as the basis for feedback, challenge, and compensation to be discussed in the next chapters.

| EXAMPLE – Spouse Job Description Monthly Planning Worksheet | | | | | | | | | |
|---|---|---|---|---|---|---|---|---|---|
| Job Category / Task: | A | B | C | D | E | F | G | H | I | J |
| | His | Hers | Ours | Rotate | Negotiate | Outsource | Neither | Don't know | # of Hours | Est. $ Cost |
| CHILDREN | | | | | | | | | | |
| changing diapers | | | √ | | | | | | 2 | $35 |
| ensuring children perform their chores | √ | | | | | | | | | |
| HOUSEHOLD CHORES | | | | | | | | | | |
| maintaining computer, printers | | | | | | | | √ | 3 | $20 |
| cleaning the bathroom | | | | | √ | | | | 4 | $50 |
| ERRANDS | | | | | | | | | | |
| dry cleaning | √ | | | | | | | | 1 | $125 |
| taking care of prescriptions | | | | | | √ | | | | $35 |
| FOOD | | | | | | | | | | |
| buying groceries | | | | | √ | | | | 2 | $500 |

| | | | | | | | | | | |
|---|---|---|---|---|---|---|---|---|---|---|
| cooking | | | | √ | | | | | 9 | $100 |
| **FINANCES** | | | | | | | | | | |
| paying bills | | √ | | | | | | | 2 | n/a |
| banking | | | | √ | | | | | 1 | n/a |
| **PETS** | | | | | | | | | | |
| veterinary care for pets | | | | | | √ | | | 1 | $10 |
| washing the dog | | | √ | | | | | | 1 | n/a |
| **FAMILY MANAGEMENT** | | | | | | | | | | |
| planning trips & vacations | | | √ | | | | | | 1 | n/a |
| maintaining family calendar | | | | | | | | √ | 1 | n/a |

## Delegating, Outsourcing, and Re-Prioritizing

Job descriptions change over time and with evolving situations. A restaurant manager may have fundamentally the same job but radically different tasks when his staff changes from five to fifteen employees. Likewise in your marriage: you might be in charge of cars, lawn care, and snow removal but when you move from an apartment, which takes care of most of that, to a house, where you are personally responsible for all of it, then the tasks required of you change. Sometimes the change is temporary, like if you just had back surgery and can't be in charge of maintenance for eight weeks. Other times the change is more permanent, such as when one spouse or another develops a chronic health problem. The important thing is that you figure out how to get the task done, or whether or not in your new life situation it even needs to be done, and how best to see to it.

Beyond just simple delegation of tasks you may want to consider "outsourcing." Many companies outsource to external vendors all of those tasks which are not deemed "mission-critical." It is okay to do the same in your marriage. Technology can go a long way to making your life easier. Internet resources, smartphone apps, and social media have made readily available a whole host of goods and services that you and your spouse can benefit from, especially if you can't agree on who should do it.

Some of these things you are probably doing already, like online banking and bill paying, but some of them may be worth looking into: in-home chefs, a dog walker, part-time nannies and handymen. Making good use of these external services should not be seen simply as a frivolous expense but may well pay off in the overall health and well-being of your relationship. The point is to make choices with respect to the relationship, to your ability to grow in virtue and holiness together, and to accomplish the Vision of your marriage.

To that end, sometimes these conversations happen with too much being presumed from both parties. Thinking outside the box is important in order to keep your relationship vital, creative, and healthy. There are certain things in your life that are probably non-negotiable: finances, taxes, keeping up the property, personal care, hygiene, keeping the house clean and safe, keeping the kids fed and cared for, etc. But as you grow older, and the relationship grows and changes, some of these categories may change too. What this means is that tasks change over time, and so therefore do job descriptions. Bringing your job descriptions on your annual couple's retreat, which you will hear about later in this book, is one good way to make sure that you are keeping up with each other and with the changes in your relationship. Adjusting as necessary, even during the year, is another sign of how much care and concern you bring to the relationship.

## Conclusion

Keeping a modern marriage going can be tough and there will inevitably be disappointments and unmet expectations. There is no need, however, to make the already trying task of negotiating marriage and family life harder by being less than clear with your spouse about what you expect from them or by simply playing a game of mind reader with your spouse every time they seem to want something. Your marriage is more than that. It is a living, breathing, teeming reality, one that is full of passion, love, hope, adventure, and dreams you haven't even dreamed yet. Written Job Descriptions with clear expectations, along with regular review, consistent challenge, and improvement are how, together, you can protect this hope-filled future and help make it a reality in the present.

## Recap

- What does a successful marital job description look like?
- What are reasonable expectations for both parties? How do you plan on handling conflict over misplaced expectations?
- How can the job description, used in conjunction with the Vision Statement, provide a helpful framework for holding one another accountable to the values of the marriage?
- How can delegation, outsourcing, and reprioritizing help you protect what's truly important in your marriage?
- How does having clear expectations concerning the marriage impact your relationship now?

# CHAPTER 7:
## Compensation and Benefits

*"In fact, when we were with you, we instructed you that if anyone was unwilling to work, neither should that one eat."*
*— 2 Thessalonians 3:10*

*"You know you are on the road to success if you would do your job, and not be paid for it." — Oprah Winfrey*

Like every organization, funding operations is only part of the story. You also need to take care of your employees. That is, you need to be clear with each other about what your compensation and benefits package looks like. Not sure of the connection to marriage? How about this: you need to be clear just what you're both in this relationship for and what motivates you to work to accomplish your Vision. In short, how do you both compensate and benefit one another in the regular course of your relationship to grow the love between you?

This chapter is all about motivations: what motivates you, what motivates your partner, and how you can work together to help motivate each other to work through the more challenging parts of married life. For this to be effective it's going to require some very hard work from both of you and, as always, an immense amount of trust in your spouse.

## Chapter Objectives

- Understand the importance of getting paid: emotionally, personally, and spiritually.
- Name and claim those benefits which are most important to you and your spouse.
- Identify those benefits which require your special attention or which don't come especially easy to you.

- Form a plan for assisting your spouse in a difficult or stressful situation.

## The Importance of Getting Paid

Using a business-based model to talk about marriage can make it easier (especially for men) to engage in an open, honest discussion about how to increase the level of success in your marriage. When we go to work we get paid, but what is the equivalent currency in a marriage?

If you grew up in a positive, loving home where Dad was the one who worked and Mom stayed home to tend the kids and house, consciously or not, you will be motivated to try and recreate the same reality for you and your spouse, even if consciously you claim you are not. Likewise, if you came from a dysfunctional, abusive, alcoholic home then your tendency might be to try and make a life for yourself and your spouse as different from that as possible.

Recognize that different things motivate different people, and that popular stereotypes, gender profiling, and perhaps even your own sense of your spouse before you married might not be totally accurate. The point is that you need to figure out what actually works for you and for your partner and you can't really do that without talking to each other about it.

## Emotional Paychecks

In the business world, a person's salary is usually determined based upon the value of their contribution to the company's bottom line. In the world of your marriage the situation is not so different: both you and your partner add value to the relationship based upon the specific tasks, skill sets, and contributions you make to the household and to the way in which you fulfill your job description. For that reason it can be really helpful for you to figure out the relative monetary value that you bring to the relationship.

Start with the job description you two worked out in the previous chapter and look at the tasks you agreed would be your responsibility.

Now note how much time you spend on those tasks each month and the estimated amount of money it would cost to have someone else perform the same service for you.

Perfect accuracy is not the point here, though it's important to be as reasonable with your assessment as you can by using the Relationship Compensation Worksheet below. Unless you're looking at retooling your job descriptions it probably doesn't matter if the going rate for lawn care is $20 an hour or $30. What does matter is that together you come to see that you both contribute and derive value from the relationship. This is true across the board which is why, in your marriage, a spouse that stays at home and takes primary responsibility for the children ought to be valued as much as one that brings in a six figure salary when you consider what it would cost to buy the services they provide on the market.

| Relationship Compensation – Calculation Worksheet | | |
|---|---|---|
| SAMPLES | | |
| Task | Monthly cost | Annual Cost |
| House cleaning—maid service | $100 - $200 | $1,200 - $2,400 |
| Chauffeur—family & children | $400 - $600 | $4,800 - $7,200 |
| Automobile care & maintenance | $50 - $200 | $600 - $2,400 |
| Personal assistant—maintaining schedule, run errands, buying gifts, event planning, etc. | $1,000 - $2,000 | $12,000 - $24,000 |
| Nanny—daycare | $1,600 - $2,000 | $19,200 - $24,000 |
| Yard work—gardening | $90 - $120 | $1,080 - $1,440 |
| Bookkeeper—maintaining personal finances: includes banking, financial software, taxes | $100 - $300 | $1,200 - $3,600 |

Of course, to the outside world this may seem crazy. We don't pay babysitters, maids, or cooks six figure salaries; but, if we valued the care of our children and homes the way we should, we'd probably be treating them a lot better too. The point is that, just as in business, there are certain values which cannot be easily quantified. A spouse who works from the home and only makes half of what his wife does working full time might be valued for his creativity, the way he has rehabbed the house, and his lessons homeschooling the children.

Make your own Relationship Compensation Worksheet to help you map out your contribution. This should have at least three effects: First, it should help you see just how much you and your spouse contribute to this partnership. Second, it should give you both a sense of just how much work you really put into this, even when you're struggling, just to make it work. Finally, it should give you both a real sense of accomplishment. Look at how much you've already done just by maintaining yourselves for however long you've been together. Imagine, then, just what you might be capable of if you engaged this more purposefully.

## Benefits Package

Besides the emotional paychecks, then, you need to explore your collective benefits package. At work your benefits might include health and dental insurance, 401Ks, educational opportunities, travel, expense accounts, a company car, maternity leave, PTO, flex hours, and working some time from home. Beyond these formalized benefits your work might give you an increased sense of self-worth, a feeling of camaraderie between you and your colleagues, and a chance to continue to grow personally and professionally.

The same should apply to your marriage. You should feel good about it, have a better sense of both yourself and your partner, and rest assured in the knowledge that you are in fact improving each other by giving fully to the relationship. The benefits are, of course, different. Perhaps the major benefit is simply the knowledge and experience of being loved wholly, absolutely, and unconditionally by another. A satisfying sex life is also an important benefit of your marriage. Daily companionship, someone to vent to, a partner in projects, and a confidante with whom to share your hopes and dreams might also be among the benefits which you find you value most. Some things might be very specific to your partnership: someone to ski with, someone to play cribbage with, an adventurous travel partner, a skilled debate partner, and so on. Certainly in our context one of the major benefits, which should also be wrapped up in the overall "paycheck" which you receive and the major purpose of the relationship to start off with, is a supportive partner in the Faith. If everything is working right, you should be coming to know God better and love Him more because of your relationship with your spouse and the same should be true for them as well.

For this reason, having drawn up the chart of the various contributions which you both make to the relationship, it may be helpful at this point to begin to list some of these specific benefits. You could just use some bullet points under a heading such as "Benefits of Being Married to You," and then list things like: a father for my children, a life full of travel and adventure, a love for fine food, secure income and financial future, well-planned retirement, etc. As you find yourself listing off the components of the benefits package, highlight or mark the items which you value most. Pay attention to the benefits your partner values as well. This will help you both understand better what best motivates your spouse in the relationship, especially when things get tough.

Because the benefits package is so individual it probably makes sense to make your lists separately and then come back together to go over them and combine them. As you discuss them, however, think about the way you would negotiate with a potential new employer. How would you articulate those benefits which you desire most and which would best enable you to do your job? For instance, a membership in the corporate gym might be a great perk of working somewhere. But if you don't actually use the gym, and reasonably know that you won't, then it probably shouldn't be high up in your benefits' list. Likewise in your marriage. If a certain amount of time apart being built into each day is important to you (as it likely will be for most introverts), then make sure your partner knows why this benefit is ranked three ahead of bi-weekly sex and two behind regular trips to your in-laws. In general, here are some principles to consider:

- What would be your preferred form of recognition or compensation for your contribution to the relationship? What is your preferred emotional paycheck? In what ways are you willing to offer your spouse theirs?

- What ways do you like for your partner to show they love you? Do you like surprises? Gifts? Unplanned trips? Doing your chores for you? How do you prefer they ask before doing something?

- How do you prefer to celebrate special events (birthdays, anniversaries, holidays, etc.)? Do you have special rules for gifts, preparing special foods, or inviting outside guests?

- What are you comfortable with regarding physical affection (in public and in private)?

- When you do something which benefits the relationship in a notable way, how would you like to be recognized and your accomplishment acknowledged?

- When you are stressed, under pressure, or otherwise put out, how would you like your partner to express support?

These questions should help you frame a more formal benefits package. Unlike some of the other documents this one should be fairly fluid as needs and wants change over time. Once completed, however, it should be something which you and your spouse revisit periodically (say, once or twice a year), just to make sure that everyone continues to be clear about expectations.

## Contracts and Covenants

The purpose of these concrete activities in *The Mission of Love*—the job descriptions, the emotional paychecks, compensation, benefits and such—is to have you consider the ultimate activity of writing a "Relationship Covenant." The idea here is not to come up with a contractual, legalistic pre-nuptial or post-nuptial agreement; in fact, the Church considers such documents objectively problematic because they presume that the marriage is in fact breakable. This is instead a kind of written-down summary of the general expectations which both of you have concerning your marriage. It is a way to put down in concrete terms exactly what you are saying "I do" to through the demands and growth of your life together. The main purpose in generating this document is to provide you both with a tool by which you can hold one another accountable to your Vision Statement.

Covenants are something like contracts but are also something much, much more. They do involve mutual obligations but they are not primarily legal agreements; they are personal and spiritual agreements. The first covenant that God makes is with Adam/humankind in general. It involves the command to be fruitful and multiply (God actually commands us to make love; so much for the Church hating sex, huh?), to be good stewards of creation, and not to eat from the tree of knowledge of good and evil, because marriage, as a covenant, is a sacramental witness of God's own love for us.

So, if you would like to take a big step in deepening your marital commitment and increasing emotional intimacy with your partner, gather up the materials you've produced thus far: your Vision Statement, Coat of Arms, Relationship Motto, Job Descriptions, and Benefit and Compensation plans, and write out a Relationship Covenant. Include things like: a list of needs and wants, expectations, hopes, and ideals for the particular facets of your relationship. A possible format has been provided below:

# Relationship Covenant

My name:
My Spouse's Name:

A general statement regarding the nature, purpose, and vision of your marriage.

**Money** – A general statement of your financial philosophy and principles guiding the spending of money, tithing, and charitable contributions.

**Sex** – Name what you think sex is for and how it is to be lived out in your marriage. Make as clear as necessary what is and what is not out-of-bounds, sexually speaking. Be sensitive to the sexual desires of your spouse.

**Careers** – Articulate the reason for each person working. Is it about money? Personal satisfaction? Accomplishing some sort of goal? Relate this to the financial and personal state of the family. Are both of you going to work? If so, why? If not, why not? How will you decide when one person is to stop working and for how long? How will you make decisions about relocating or radically changing lifestyles for careers? How will you make decisions about the choice to switch careers?

**Children** – What is your philosophy of childhood and childrearing? How will you decide when/if to have children? What duties and responsibilities will each partner take on relative to children? How will decisions be made about schools, extra-curriculars, and discipline?

**Families/In-Laws** – What is your attitude towards each other's family? How will you coordinate holidays, special events, and other visits? How will ethnic and cultural traditions from either side play into the life of your family?

**Residences** – Where will you live? How will you decide the type of housing? Who will be responsible for which kinds of maintenance? How will decisions regarding changes to these decisions be made?

**Friends** – What are your attitudes towards friends which you both have from before? What about the friends you "share" as a couple? What sort of boundaries or expectations do you have regarding new friends and their involvement in your life together? Are there different rules/boundaries if the friends in question are members of the opposite sex? What rules will you have regarding old boy-friends/girlfriends?

**Recreation** – How will you share recreation? How will you each maintain your own kind of recreation? Will there be built-in periods of "guy time" or "gal time" for each of you? How will you communicate the need to recreate alone in a way which only minimally alienates your spouse?

**Religion** – Do you share the same faith? If not, how will you negotiate that together? How will you ensure that you do not interfere in the other's practice of their faith? How will you raise the children? How will you make sure to pass on the Faith to them? What are the expectations regarding regular Mass attendance, prayers before meals, and other special time? How will you put your faith into action? What sorts of volunteer and charitable opportunities will you participate in together? Separately? How will you commit to supporting one another spiritually and challenging each other as appropriate? How will you decide together how much to contribute of time, talent, and treasure?

**General Conflicts** – What kind of problem-solving techniques do you commit to employing when things get rough? Will you plan for a mandatory cool-down period after each argument before trying to have a discussion again (this may not be necessary but, in some cases, can save marriages)? Would you both agree in principal to counseling? Who are you comfortable having your spouse talk to about your marriage? Who are you uncomfortable having them share with? Why? What will you both commit to doing which will minimize unnecessary conflict and negotiate fruitfully inevitable conflict?

The marriage vows themselves establish a covenant, a personal self-donation to your spouse. The limitation with the marital vows is that often times the specific behavioral features of the relationship are left unsaid. That which is unsaid is often unclear and so you and your spouse can coexist for a long time in honest ignorance or confusion about one another's expectations. This covenant should help you put most, if not all, of your expectations, fears, hopes, worries, concerns, joys, and dreams for your marriage out on the table. Only by being completely open and honest with each other do you stand a real chance of helping the other grow in holiness and so accomplish the Vision of your marriage.

## Recap

- What motivates your partner? How can you be more attentive to their needs? Are there ways during peak periods that you can better motivate them?
- What benefits do you get from your relationship? Are you grateful for them? Do you thank your partner?
- What is the difference between a contract and a covenant? Why is it important for Christian couples in a sacramental marriage to see their relationship primarily from the perspective of a covenant?

# Book III: Why?

In the first section of the book we laid out a basic vision of marriage as the Church understands it. In the second we showed you what healthy Christian marriages look like. Now, in the third and final section of the book, we want to provide tools that will help remind you, as a couple, why all of this work was so important to begin with.

What we aim to do here is make explicit what was implicit throughout the book thus far. Most of us in most of our relationships make all sorts of presumptions about why we do what we do and why everyone else does what they do. But if we are to be truly intentional in our marriages as Christians then we are called in an explicit way to be clear about what we're doing together—as a couple. That is the reason for the Vision Statement and Branding, why Job Descriptions with clear expectations are essential, and why Financial Serenity is so important to strive for. The love you have is worth protecting and all of the tools and resources we've given you here are meant to enable you to do just that.

What follows is a reminder of what's possible and of why you first believed anything is possible with the love of your life. It combines the grand theology of the first book with the practical wisdom of the second to sketch out *The Mission of Love*—an open and honest plan of how to live your life together as married Christians. But this "reminder" is no less important than the other tasks before it. Just because you have a purpose for your marriage and a plan for fulfilling it does not mean you will never grow weary or weak in striving to accomplish it; even Christ needed Simon to help carry His cross. You will need time to refresh, realign, and even heal throughout your journey together. Of course, the value in what follows lies in your ability and willingness to make it your own. That's what we mean to help you do and that's what we hope you'll do for each other.

# CHAPTER 8:
## A Sacramental People

*"He has willed to make men holy and save them, not as individuals without any bond or link between them, but rather to make them into a people who might acknowledge him and serve him in holiness."*
*— Vatican II, Lumen Gentium, 9*

One of the most important differences between the Church and any other organization, besides professing some common set of values or ideals, is that the Church claims that by initiation into it the person is forever changed.

For example, holy baptism is the basis of the whole Christian life, the gateway to life in the Spirit and the door which gives access to the other sacraments. Through baptism we are freed from sin and reborn as sons of God, we become members of Christ, and we are incorporated into the Church and made sharers in her mission: "Baptism is the sacrament of regeneration through water and in the word" (*Catholic Church* 1213). It imprints on the soul an indelible spiritual sign, the character, which consecrates the baptized person for Christian worship and literally makes the person, even as a little baby, into a new creation. That whole person's life is different now no matter what, even if they choose to later reject the gift which they have received. So from the very beginning the people who celebrate sacraments, including marriage, find themselves a sacramental people.

## Chapter Objectives

- Articulate how membership in the Church is different than membership in any other organization. Why are marriages among Christians, therefore, different than among other people?
- Give examples of grace in the life of the Christian couple and especially of the natural ways our family lives parallel the sacraments.

- Explain the role of parish involvement and regular reception of the sacraments in the life of Christian couples.

A member of any purely human organization can basically enter and leave at will. Even other groups which have initiation rituals, like the Masons, don't profess to be fundamentally changing the soul of the person brought in—but that is precisely what the Church claims to be doing.

Marriage between Baptized persons is sacramental and a continuation of that initiation into the life of the Church. Unlike a strictly legal or natural marriage, a sacramental marriage is not a human institution and a person cannot enter and leave at will. As Christ says to the Pharisees, "what God has joined together, no human being must separate" (Mk 10:9). A sacramental people in marriage have become channels of God's grace, of the divine life itself, both to one another and to the world. By your vocation, you have become a "domestic Church" with a mission not only for your own family but, on a much higher level, for the participation and advancement of the Kingdom of God here on earth as part of the Church universal. The spiritual health of the entire Catholic Church is dependent upon the Holy Spirit and His work through every baptized member of Christ's Body entrusted with this same mission; we must be as holy as we want the Church to be if it is to truly flourish.

## Tuning In

Sacraments "make present the grace they signify." Grace is kind of a funny word. It's a lot like gravity; people use it a lot but it's not always clear what they mean by it, and often enough it seems they don't know themselves. The *Catechism* says this:

> Grace is first and foremost the gift of the Spirit who justifies and sanctifies us. But grace also includes the gifts that the Spirit grants us to associate us with his work, to enable us to collaborate in the salvation of others and in the growth of the Body of Christ, the Church (*Catholic Church* 2003).

The Holy Spirit enables us to share the gift of God's life which we've been given. This is why in the nuptial blessing—that special blessing you received from the priest on the day of your wedding—there's an explicit *epiclesis* or calling down of the Holy Spirit. So part of what makes a Christian marriage different from any other is what it signifies, the "something more" that it represents. But even more is the means that it uses to get there—for the Holy Spirit of God Himself dwells at the heart of a Christian marriage, is the firm foundation of the Christian family, and that is what enables us to accomplish our mission together.

So what does that look like in real life? Well there are three primary ways that the Holy Spirit helps us act as channels of grace in our marriage. First, the sacrament of marriage is the specific source and original means of sanctification for Christian married couples and families. It takes up again and makes specific the sanctifying grace of baptism. By virtue of the mystery of the death and resurrection of Christ, of which the spouses are made part in a new way by marriage, conjugal love is purified and made holy: "This love the Lord has judged worthy of special gifts, healing, perfecting and exalting gifts of grace and of charity" (John Paul II, *Familiaris Consortio*, 56).

So the first is the way in which the Spirit enables us to live our daily lives together. Can people live together in relative peace and happiness without the Holy Spirit? Sure, most of our secular friends do that all of the time. But the Holy Spirit enables us to do so in a preeminent way and supplies special graces specifically for the purpose of helping to perfect one another. This is what we mean when we say things like, "You make me want to be a better man" or "better woman."

The second help that the Spirit gives us concerns our kids. The responsibility of Christian parenthood is a serious one. Besides having to care for the material needs of the children, socialize them, educate them, and prepare them for the world in general, Christian parents also have the responsibility to pass on the Faith to their children.

> Christian marriage and the Christian family build up the Church: for in the family the human person is not only brought

into being and progressively introduced by means of education into the human community, but by means of the rebirth of baptism and education in the Faith the child is also introduced into God's family, which is the Church (John Paul II, *Familiaris Consortio,* 15).

Parents are the first formators of their children in the Faith. By word and example Christian parents pass on the Faith to their kids. This doesn't mean that every Christian has to be an amateur theologian or every fun activity with your kids has to be drawn from a CCD class, but it does mean that you have to know your faith at least reasonably well and pass it on in a clear, consistent, and appropriate way to your kids. For many of us this may mean brushing up on the Faith ourselves, either because our own formation was kind of poor or because we may have been away from the Faith for a time. It also means that we have a serious obligation, first to have our kids baptized, and second to see that they are properly catechized and receive the other sacraments as appropriate. Parents are responsible for the whole education and formation of their children: intellectual, spiritual, moral, and psychological. Of particular importance here is educating your kids in human sexuality. This doesn't begin with the "Birds and the Bees" talk at puberty, it begins right now as you relate to one another as man and woman and show your kids what a healthy, holy, happy marriage looks like.

A major component of this whole education piece is example. You won't suddenly become perfect people when you become parents. In fact, if you're like most everybody else, you'll probably come to realize just how *imperfect* you are precisely by being somebody's spouse and parent. At the same time, your example needs to match your words. If you're trying to instill honesty in your children and you keep cheating on your taxes, then you kid is going to find out, they're going to be hurt, and ultimately they're going to be resentful that you held them to a standard that you couldn't keep yourself. As kids grow they will learn to be discerning of regular and habitual faults and of serious moral problems. "Dad has a temper" produces a very different moral sense in a child than "Dad cheats on Mom." This is true also with regard to the

Church directly. You can't send kids to Catholic school and then expect the school to just "take care of" the faith dimension of your child's life. Few things are more destructive to the Church than parents sending their kids to Catholic school and then refusing to take them to Mass on Sunday. It sends mixed messages to the child and forces them, at far too young an age, to have to choose between love of their parents and the Church.

This is why the third help of the Holy Spirit to Christian couples pertains to the Church directly. Because Holy Matrimony draws its grace from the source of all grace—the passion, death, resurrection, and ascension of Jesus—it is meant to bring you *in your marriage* into deeper relationship with the Church. It means getting to Sunday Mass regularly now if you haven't been for a while. It means frequenting the sacrament of Penance (Confession) regularly now, especially if that hasn't been part of your life before. It means registering at and meaningfully belonging to a parish and taking part in its life: joining a Bible study, helping to serve the poor, volunteering at the cook out, or teaching CCD. It means offering yourself for service at the Church and utilizing the natural and developed gifts which you have in particular for the work of the Church. If you're an accountant then offer to sit on the finance council. If you're a groundskeeper then ask to help keep the landscaping up. If you have musical talents join the choir or ask to play at Mass. The bottom line is that the Holy Spirit wants to help you transform society but He doesn't expect you to do so all on your own, or even just as a couple.

## Family Sacraments

The Scriptures use a host of images to talk about God's relationship to His people. He is a shepherd and we are the sheep (Ez 34:11-4; Ps 80:1-10); He is the Lord of armies (1 Sm 1:3); He is the healer (Ex 15: 26); He is the potter and we are the clay (Isaiah 64:8); and He is the great king (Zep 3:15; Ps 24:7). Of all of the metaphors used to describe this relationship, however, two dominate: spousal love and family life.

God is called "husband" with respect to Israel his "bride" in any number of places, but two important instances to consider are the book of Hosea and the Song of Songs (also called the Song of Solomon). Hosea is considered one of the "minor" prophets. His story is a powerful one. God instructs him to marry a prostitute, which he does, and she promptly leaves him to go and sleep around with other men. But Hosea doesn't give up on his wife. He finds her and brings her back. This was an image of Israel at the time, for the nation was making alliances with other countries and falling into idolatry, thus chasing after other men. But Hosea didn't give up on Gomer (his wife), and neither will God give up on His people.

The Song of Songs is probably the most poetic book of the Bible. It is certainly the most erotic. It is essentially a love song between the king (ostensibly Solomon) and his bride (Sheba). This is a good book for couples to read together. It takes some very fleshy imagery and talks about the way God cares for his people. It should also give couples a sense of how to care for each other.

But just as with human couples, the marriage of God and Israel, of Christ and His Church, ultimately bears fruit in children. God is called a "Father" to Israel in the Old Testament, but the familial dynamic is only made clear with the coming of Christ. He teaches us to pray "Our Father" (Mt 6:9-13; Lk 11:2-5); He identifies his disciples as brother and sister and mother in relation to Himself (Mt 12:50); and Jesus is time and again referred to as "Son" in relation to the Father. The whole of the Christian life is seen as coming to be by grace (gift) what Jesus is by nature. Jesus is God the Son from all eternity, never was not God, and has always been in perfect communion with the Father. His work on earth enabled us to share in that relationship, so that the Church, the Body of Christ, is now the household of God on earth, God's own human family.

The upshot of all this is twofold: first, it gives us a sense of how our families ought to act; second, it affirms the fact that precisely in our daily lives together we come to encounter God. Family is a sacramental reality, it is the place where we encounter the grace of God.

In matrimony and in the family a complex of interpersonal relationships is set up—married life, fatherhood and motherhood, filiation and fraternity—through which each human person is introduced into the "human family" and into the "family of God," which is the Church.

Christian marriage and the Christian family build up the Church: for in the family the human person is not only brought into being and progressively introduced by means of education into the human community, but by means of the rebirth of baptism and education in the Faith the child is also introduced into God's family, which is the Church. (John Paul II, *Familiaris Consortio,* 15)

This means that the family is a "school of charity" and a "house of formation" in Christian spirituality. You will teach your kids not only how to be a man or a woman, a contributing member of society, a good citizen and a good student, but, most fundamentally, a good Christian. These lessons are not mostly taught by the priest from the pulpit but by the mom and the dad from across the kitchen table, the grandmother in the living room, and the uncle on a hike. Our families are "domestic churches" where, as in our parish church, God is worshipped, the world is prayed for, forgiveness and reconciliation are offered and received, the sick are tended to, the dying cared for, the young brought up, the single married, and where sacrifices are offered.

The Christian family constitutes a specific revelation and realization of ecclesial communion, and for this reason too it can and should be called "the domestic Church" (John Paul II, *Familiaris Consortio,* 58).

All members of the family, each according to his or her own gift, have the grace and responsibility of building, day by day, the communion of persons, making the family "a school of deeper humanity": this happens where there is care and love for the little ones, the sick, the aged; where there is mutual service every day; when there is a sharing of goods, of joys and of sorrows (John Paul II, *Familiaris Consortio,* 21).

Your family life, then, is populated by sacraments. The birth of a new child should be celebrated with joy. Coming of age and attaining manhood or womanhood should likewise be marked as significant occasions and the passing over of adult responsibility. When a member is sick we should care for them, sad we should console them. When it comes time for one of our members to marry we should greet the occasion with great joy. When we commit a serious sin against one of our own we need to ask forgiveness and we need to forgive in kind generously. Most fundamentally, we have to spend time together. Taking your kids to Mass on Sunday will be totally unintelligible if you don't eat with them during the week. Mark out special occasions: birthdays, anniversaries, deathdays, holidays, feasts, patron saints' days, and other occasions with special foods, games, and prayers. Use both of your ethnic and national traditions as a resource here to help pass on a sense of identity to your kids.

Most importantly, associate each of these with your actual experience of the Church. Go to Mass together on feast days and then come home and have an actual feast. When you go to confession together as a family do something afterwards to celebrate that reconciliation: go out for ice cream, or play a game together, or spend time with the one whom you offended. Make Sunday a genuinely special day. Even if you're in a situation where one or the other of you has to work on Sundays, on the hours you're not working, do something to tell yourselves and your kids that this day is special. Sunday's meal, and/or any other holy day's during the week should be the best of the whole week. Make sure you eat it at the table, without the television on, and intentionally spending your time together. These things will not only help your children to understand the Seven Sacraments of the Faith better, but will become occasions for real grace and conversion themselves. They also will be the day-to-day basis by which you find yourself being more and more converted to Christ and come closer and closer to accomplishing your Mission.

# The Parish As Family

Probably the word "parish" and "church" are more or less synonymous for you. They are for most Catholics. Their "parish" or "parish church" is like a little connection to the larger, upper-case "C" Church worldwide. That's not a bad start, but it's important that we don't get a sense of our parishes as just societies of like-minded people or ideological comfort zones. The Church is like the soul of humanity, it exists equally everywhere that human beings find themselves, but it organizes itself based mostly on geography. Church provinces are called "dioceses" and some important dioceses are called "archdioceses." The head of a diocese is a bishop, of an archdiocese an archbishop. Each diocese or archdiocese is further divided into parishes, and the pastor is the head of the local parish. But the parish isn't just the church building; the parish is the territory and, most especially, the people in it. By default, then, we all "belong" to the parish we live in, which is usually the Catholic Church physically nearest to us.

Not all that long ago we took this whole parish territory thing *extremely* seriously. You couldn't even satisfy your Sunday obligation in a neighboring parish without permission from both pastors. As the world has gotten more global, however, and as people tend to travel more, as a rule these restrictions have been largely relaxed. One can "join" a parish other than the one in which they are "zoned" by registering there. This is not such a bad thing: very often people have good reasons to attend another parish. For example, some people may live somewhere during the week and stay somewhere else on the weekends, or maybe the church closest to work is easier to get to during the week than the one nearest your home, or maybe you take your ailing mother to Mass each week and so by default wind up considering that place "your parish." The downside to this, though, is that our parishes can simply become places to be affirmed in all of my ideas, prejudices, and preconceptions. The identity of the parish can become about ideology or church practice and not about the Faith. This is terribly dangerous, both for the local parish which falls prey to the temptation and to the Church as a whole.

One of the most important things that you will do as a couple is choose a parish. You may have to do this any number of times, especially if you move around a lot. The first time you do it should probably be before you marry. There was a time when it was customary to get married in the bride's home parish, and this is still a perfectly legitimate custom, but it is also a very good thing as a new couple to find your own spiritual home which may very well not be where your parents or your spouse's parents still live. Start with your local parish, it may suit you fine. It may be that you are the only people under sixty in the congregation; that could be more of a problem. You may or may not like the music. You may or may not like the priest. None of these are, by themselves, entirely legitimate reasons to switch parishes. If the priest, personally, is problematic enough to get you to switch parishes then the time has probably come to write a letter to the bishop. But there may be perfectly good reasons *not* to join the parish nearest you. If you have children or are planning on having them soon and intend to send them to Catholic school then you probably need to join the parish at the school, whether that's the one closest to you or not. If one or the other works at the parish or at the school, that's another very good reason to belong to a parish outside of where you live. As you two discern this together think again about your Vision Statement and which community you think will best support you in all of this. Ask the pastor or some other priest whom you trust to help sort this out. They'll be happy to: it's why you call them "Father."

It's interesting to note that the word "parish" comes from the word "parishioner" and not the other way round. The word comes from the Greek *paroikos*, which is where we also get our English word *pariah*. It means literally "alongside the house" or "outcast," but is usually translated as "resident alien." It's the Church's way of reminding us that we are to be in the world but not of the world. The *parish* is the home of the resident aliens. It's the place where we come to remember who we really are, what we're really for, and where we're really going. The ultimate question you have to ask when trying to figure out which parish to belong to is: Do these people help support me in my effort to be a good spouse and parent? Are they helping me grow in holiness, love of God and fidelity to His Church? Are they challenging me to be more and better than I am today? If so, then you've probably found the place you need to be.

## All in the Family

"Family" is of course a pretty dynamic concept. It includes, depending upon time and context, not only one's immediate family but the whole host of secondary relations who may or may not live with someone, share time and space with them, and be related by blood, marriage, or friendship. These other members of your "family" are important both for you, your spouse, and your kids.

Hillary Clinton popularized the African proverb, "It takes a village to raise a child," and it's pretty sage advice. Parents are certainly the primary caretakers of their children and formators in the Faith but they are not the only ones. Siblings also share intimately and directly in the lives of their brothers and sisters. Many of us have wounds from our childhood because of the relationship which we may have had with our siblings. We should be careful not to perpetuate the same mistakes ourselves, but at the same time to not make new mistakes that simply tend in the opposite direction.

Grandparents have a kind of pride of place in terms of other relatives. More and more studies are showing the importance of grandparents in a child's life. As our parents age they teach us, and our children, how to grow older. They teach us about diminishment, dignity, and the wisdom that comes from old age. If your children don't have access to their grandparents because of distance, or because you are estranged, or because your parents have already passed on, be intentional about forming relationships with other old people. These "surrogate grandparents" can be a tremendous influence not only on your child's life but on yours as well.

Some parishes and Newman Centers will actually pair up young couples, especially if they are living far from home, with an older couple in order to ask for advice and have good role models. This can be especially helpful early on in a marriage when boundaries, finances, sex, and religion often need to be negotiated and re-negotiated. Talking the trouble through with someone who has been there before can be incredibly helpful.

Aunts, uncles, and cousins are also important characters in a family's life. When you consider moving for a job or for whatever reason, your relationship with your extended family ought to be part of the consideration. That's certainly not to say that everyone has to live near their relatives (the Holy Family moved to a different country), but if our relationships with our extended family don't even play into the decision then something has probably gone very wrong. Try to include the extended family as best as you are able to in those special occasions mentioned above. Not only is it good for your kids, but you and your cousins might find each other helpful resources as you both set about the task of raising your kids.

For most of us our friends, either from growing up, or from college, or from work, or some other group comprise a kind of pseudo-family. This can be true especially if we wound up settling far from our family of origin. Surrogate aunts and uncles are important in the life of your kids too. What's more, we teach our kids about friendship by the way we treat our own friends. Consider that when you struggle with your relationships outside of the family.

Finally, there are our priests and religious. Now this may seem counterintuitive; you may be thinking, "But I don't have any priests or religious in my family!" But you do. Your parish priest is a *de facto* member of every family in his parish. "Father" isn't just a title; it establishes a relationship, and your kids will learn about how to relate to the Church, to her priests, and to other Church workers by watching you. The priest you have now may not be your favorite. Fine, but your dad might be kind of a jerk too—he's still your dad. The familial character of these relationships works in two ways. First, as a member of the Church you automatically are queued into these relationships whether you want them or not. You need, at a minimum, to contribute something to their upkeep and greet them after Mass. A good priest will be involved with his people's lives. Few things bring greater joy to a priest than being invited to someone's house for dinner. Part of the reason he doesn't have a family of his own is so that he can be free to join yours. A similar dynamic is at work with religious brothers and sisters. If there are religious sisters at your parish or at the school, bring them things, tell them you appreciate their vocation, and ask them to pray for you and your special intentions. More fundamentally, when you run into real spiritual difficulty, approach the priests you trust, either your own parish priest or some other, and let him be a priest for you. It's what he's *for*, it's how you help him to accomplish his mission, and he is there to help you accomplish your own.

## Conclusion

Sacramental people have a way of being family which is different than most. Besides simply enjoying the relationships which we have and growing in human ways by coming to appreciate one another more, we are able to act as channels of grace and vehicles of God's life to one another. This happens because of the sacraments which we celebrate and the lives which we live in common. Take advantage of the relationships God has given and let them change you. This is the place you've been given to accomplish your Mission, these are the people God has given to assist you. Thank God for them and for the gift He has given you, not only to be helped by them, but to help them in return. Together, you will help each other accomplish your Mission and transform the Church.

## Recap

- How is belonging to the Church like belonging to a family?
- Why is being married in the Church different than being married outside of it?
- How does grace affect the lives of baptized married persons?
- Why is involvement in the parish an essential part of every Christian marriage? How can you best support your marriage by your involvement at the local parish?
- How can you as a couple best be of service to your local Church?

# CHAPTER 9:
## Virtue Coaching:
## Feedback, Redirect, and Reconciliation

*"If your brother sins [against you], go and tell him his fault between you and him alone. If he listens to you, you have won over your brother. If he does not listen, take one or two others along with you, so that 'every fact may be established on the testimony of two or three witnesses.' If he refuses to listen to them, tell the church..."*

*— Mt 18:15-17*

*"Christ dwells with them [Christian spouses], gives them the strength to take up their crosses and so follow him, to rise again after they have fallen, to forgive one another, to bear one another's burdens, to 'be subject to one another out of reverence for Christ,' and to love one another with supernatural, tender, and fruitful love. In the joys of their love and family life he gives them here on earth a foretaste of the wedding feast of the Lamb..."*

*— Catechism of the Catholic Church, 1642*

## Chapter Objectives

- Articulate a simple, easy, understandable definition of virtue. Be able to provide examples from daily life.
- Show how spouses are uniquely suited, and uniquely called, to be "virtue coaches" for one another.
- Devise an examination of conscience for yourself, especially in regard to your position as spouse.
- Discuss feedback in the context of relationship and why something like feedback forms can be so helpful.

## Truth-Telling

Each of us knows that he or she is imperfect but most of us don't like to be reminded of it very often. In most of our relationships we prefer to maintain the illusion of perfection, or at least pretend that we are much better at many more things than we actually are. This is ultimately the result of sin. Sin obscures our vision and prevents us from seeing ourselves and everyone else as they actually are.

Marriage is intended to help fix that. Your marriage is meant to be a safe place where you can be yourself—really and truly yourself—with the other person and not fear judgment. That isn't to say that you won't be corrected for your mistakes or challenged to improve your personal, moral, emotional, physical, and spiritual state but with your spouse at least, and hopefully with a few close family and friends, you can make yourself genuinely vulnerable in order to grow in holiness.

## The Importance of Being Virtuous

As a child you were likely taught the Ten Commandments. These are the basic moral guidelines by which not only Christians and Jews try to live but by which most other people of goodwill try to live their lives as well. The way the commandments get obeyed in real life, however, is seldom by a series of individual decisions (i.e. I have to decide *today* to not have an affair with my secretary) but rather by way of *virtue*. The word "virtue" has gotten kind of a bad rap; it conjures up images of the Church Lady from *Saturday Night Live* and puritanical prudes whose mission is to save the rest of the world from fun. But nothing could be further from the truth. The word *virtue* comes from the Latin *vir,* meaning "man." This "man" is male-specific but that doesn't mean that women can't be virtuous. It's because ancient Greek and Roman Heroes (think Perseus and Aeneas) were considered the most virtuous; that is, they were brave, strong, true, and loyal. So while the word may be related to males in the gendered sense, the idea is absolutely universal. Virtues are the habits which characterize the lives of morally good people.

You already have any number of virtues. In the example above, you have most likely developed to a certain degree both chastity and temperance. Chastity isn't just a virtue for priests or religious; it doesn't mean simply "not having sex," but rather "living out my sexuality in accord with my state in life." In that way a married woman can be said to rightfully have "chaste sex" with her husband. She has the virtue of chastity, not because every day she has to constantly say, "Here's an available guy that I could probably seduce or whom I know is after me but I'm going to consciously think about *not* having sex with him." No, rather, the virtue is what allows for her to live a normal day-to-day life without having to do that at all. The virtue is the habit of love and fidelity that she has first to her husband, and in a secondary way the habit of love, friendliness, and care which she has for the other men in her life who likewise benefit from her chastity because they are not tempted to sin themselves.

Virtue is not something which happens overnight nor is it something that one gets without any work. Growth in virtue happens over a long period of time, as do all habits, and require attention and consistency. Since one of the major duties of your spouse (and therefore one of your major duties as well) is to help your partner overcome sin and grow into the sort of person they were always meant to be, *Virtue Coaching* will be one of the most important things which you do for one another.

## Virtue in the Mean

"There's a right way and a wrong way to do everything," the saying begins, and then follows up with whatever the speaker's account of the right and wrong way might be. In truth, most things don't simply have a right and a wrong way of being done but there are typically better and worse ways of doing them. Coaching your partner in virtue and challenging them in deeply personal ways is no different. A lot of this will depend upon you and your spouse, your personalities and your relationship. At the same time, there are some overall ways in which one can be a good or a bad coach.

At this stage you may be getting a little bit nervous. Even if you grew up in a pretty healthy family, typically one partner in a marriage is more critical than the other, or at least one is more open in voicing their concerns. She's a nag; he's a boar. Neither one is what we're going for here. But the fear over nagging isn't just crazy. Few things militate against a good and pleasant marriage more than hyper-criticism. Typically this happens because, as a couple, you have not set good boundaries around when, where, and how feedback is to be given and received, and how criticism is to take place. Now clearly there are times when a spouse might need to step in immediately: if someone's life, health, or welfare is at stake, if the spouse seems not to be in their right mind, or if the relationship itself and/or the children wind up being exposed to some serious harm. For instance, if you're at the company Christmas party and your spouse has too much to drink, then simply taking away the car keys or calling a cab is probably the right thing to do, even if it means they're going to be grumpy about it later. But barring extreme circumstances like that, feedback should be given in a clear and orderly way and in a safe, agreed-upon environment. This will both minimize the possibility of embarrassment for your partner and maximize your ability to make your thoughts and feelings known, as well as maximizing their capacity to receive it.

Relationship feedback is a delicate thing. Most of us like to think that, at least generally, we are decent husbands or wives. So long as we aren't cheating on our spouse, the house isn't in jeopardy, and the kids aren't in jail, we're doing pretty good, right? Actually, those often aren't the best indicators of health in a relationship. A healthy, holy, and even happy couple can find themselves in financial straits and lose a house— but save a marriage. A good family can have a child go through a difficult stage and wind up in jail but it needn't be the end of the world. And yes, marriages can even survive infidelity, though it's very difficult and painful. The point is that the overall health and vitality of your relationship cannot be bound simply to any one goal or objective. It's about the whole package. In the end, successful feedback is too.

It's not going to be possible to have successful feedback without having done some of the background work we've talked about in this book. The Vision Statement, Job Descriptions, Relationship Objectives, and lists of responsibilities are all important for being able to provide concrete and clear feedback and so move your partner to action. "You're dirty," or "Your office is a mess," is not nearly as helpful as, "Honey, I thought we agreed that you'd clean the office at least once a week. Now it's been a whole month and nothing's been touched. Are you okay? Is there anything I can do to help? Or do we need to adjust the cleaning schedule?" Again, the major thing to avoid is simply communicating negative feelings and general annoyance; those aren't helpful and, if they're true, your partner probably knows about them already. What's more, the judgmental nature of these kinds of comments (e.g. "You're dirty") puts your partner on the defensive and will likely result in them denying or minimizing the problem rather than addressing it.

So one version of the bad coach is the negative nag. That's to be avoided. Equally problematic, however, is the conflict-averse enabler. Giving and receiving Relationship Feedback and growing into a good Virtue Coach is one of the major reasons you got married. So while it looks like you're the one helping your partner grow in virtue be providing them with challenge and critique, it should actually be helping you grow in virtue by confronting your fear of conflict and growing in courage and valor. Fear of conflict is an absolute detriment to a healthy marriage. Conflict is inevitable. The point of a healthy, holy, and happy marriage is to learn to negotiate and facilitate conflict in creative, productive, and constructive ways.

The conflict-averse enabler makes for a bad spouse because they leave their spouse in their sins and failings. Putting up with one another's failings and inadequacies is part of how a spouse grows in virtue and holiness, by developing more patience, having the grace to see God's design in less than perfect situations, and hopefully becoming more merciful to one's self and others. But permitting bad, destructive, dysfunctional, and unhealthy behavior to continue is not loving. It is, in fact, unhealthy, dysfunctional, destructive, and bad in itself—in short, it's just another kind of sin.

So a good Virtue Coach starts with honesty. Making a little examination of conscience a couple of times a day can help a great deal. An examination of conscience is a kind of self-examination that we typically do before we go to confession but which all of the great spiritual writers recommend we do frequently, and even daily. You should write one specific examination for yourself because you know your own sins (think about what you usually say in confession or in close confidence with a good friend). It might look something like this:

## Sample Examination of Conscience

- Have I prayed today? When I prayed did I thank God for my spouse? Did I pray for my spouse and our relationship? Did I ask for the grace today to be more faithful than I have ever been before?

- Am I paying enough attention to my spouse? Am I taking account of their needs, anticipating desires as best as I can, and fulfilling my part in this relationship?

- (If there are children) How am I doing as a Mom/Dad? Am I providing a good example to my kids? Am I fair with discipline? Too harsh? Not stern enough? Do I let my kids see how much I love their Mom/Dad? Have I thanked God today for the gift of my children? Have I asked for their protection and help? Am I spending enough time with them?

- Am I doing my part in keeping up our household? Have I tended to all of those duties that are mine? Have I let anything slip of late? Have I been quick to correct my mistakes or get help if I needed it?

- Am I responsible with our resources? Do I spend money needlessly or frivolously? Am I doing my part to help us live within our means? Am I helping us to save for the future? Do I make sacrifices where necessary? Do I encourage my spouse/kids to do the same? Are we giving enough time, talent, and treasure both to the Church and to charity?

- Am I attentive to my partner's emotional life? Am I honest, both with myself and my spouse concerning my own personal/emotional state? Am I being fair in my expectations? Do I hold my spouse to a standard which I cannot meet myself? Do I express dissatisfaction in a way which can be heard?

- Am I attentive to the sexual needs/desires of my spouse? Am I willing to give of myself and do I feel free to ask the same of my spouse? How do I handle a negative response? Am I holding any part of myself back? Am I masturbating privately? Am I looking at pornography? When I'm with my spouse am I imagining being with somebody else? Do I work hard sexually to give of myself and not simply use my partner for my own enjoyment?

- Am I open to the gift of new life which God longs to give in our sexual expression, both in terms of children and in terms of our own relationship? Do I create space so that my partner can make their own needs, anxieties, or desires felt? Am I clear on sexual boundaries, both between ourselves and other people? Do I show my spouse appropriate affection in public, and especially in front of our children?

- Am I living my marriage at the service of the Church and of the world? Do my spouse and I set a good example of married love for our friends and neighbors? Do we give of ourselves willingly as a couple and as a family? Are we both keeping in mind the overall Vision of our Marriage? How is our love a sign of Christ's love for His Church? How could we be doing better?

Again, this is only an example. Yours could include such specific questions as, "Have I unloaded the dishwasher today?" or "Did I remind my wife about soccer practice?" These are all things which may be particular challenges in your own relationship. In any case, running through an examination of conscience each day, maybe at night before bed, maybe on your morning run, or in the car, or the shower, or at some other convenient time can be a good way to keep yourself honest and help you frame any subsequent conversation with your spouse.

Another mistake the potential Virtue Coach can make is to presume that, because they are not perfect themselves, they are in no position to offer constructive criticism to their spouse. This is an entirely natural but unnecessary worry. If someone at work is trying your patience by taking home office supplies and always clocking in late, then you are less likely to confront them if you occasionally keep paperclips and arrive late. But the situation is totally different with your spouse. Correction from a coworker can arise from, and be received with, a variety of motives. Plus, the person could feel threatened. Correction, redirection, and reconciliation in a marriage should never be met with fear or suspicion. *The reason for your marriage* is to help make you better people and, together, to help make everyone else better too. How can you hope to do that if someone—especially the someone closest to you—can't point out the places where you still have to grow? So the most important prerequisite for a Virtue Coach is to strive towards virtue yourself, not necessarily making it 100% of the time but having a coach of your own along with you to help support you, encourage you, and make you better as you go.

## Keepin' It Regular

The athletic metaphor is a good one for the spiritual life and for virtue formation in particular because virtues are a lot like athletic skills, you only get them if you use them. That sounds counterintuitive. How can you use something you don't have? A good illustration of virtue formation works like this: A little boy is afraid of the dark. He tells his dad that he's scared and can't sleep. His dad tells him to pretend to be brave. He does with all of his might and, after a few nights, he isn't afraid the dark anymore. Practice makes perfect. Each of us has the seed of all the virtues deep within us but they each just need to be exercised a bit in order to develop the habit. Paradoxically, you get to be brave by acting bravely, you acquire abstinence by repeatedly and readily abstaining, you become just by acting justly.

So, like training for a sport, you've got to keep your virtue regime regular. Meet with your coach at prearranged times and in designated places so that you both know what's coming. You wouldn't expect your coworkers to respond well if over your coffee break at the office you asked to do some weight training. Likewise, don't spring a feedback session on your spouse just after he's finished trimming the hedge. A good rule of thumb is to meet every other week. So maybe 7:00 - 7:30pm on the first and third Tuesday of the month is set aside for a Virtue Coaching feedback session.

As with practice for a sport, there should be something of a regular routine. A good "warm up" is to start with a general "check in." You probably check in with each other at the end of each day anyway but this gives the opportunity for a little more substantive reflection on the last week or two. Maybe share some highlights and challenges, and let the challenges segue naturally into the feedback.

Start with the positive feedback. Now, if your relationship is even half-healthy, you probably provide positive feedback spontaneously during the week: "Honey, you look nice today," "Thanks for mowing the lawn, Sweetheart," "You look handsome today," are all forms of positive feedback. These can and should continue, and hopefully even increase and grow in quality. But the kind of positive relationship feedback you give in one of your regular meetings should be more intentional. More than just appreciating what's going on around you, look back at their job description and articulate specifically what you're grateful for. Instead of simply saying, "The kitchen looks great," try instead, "Thank you for your care in the kitchen. The pantry is so neat and orderly and the cabinets so well organized." The more descriptive and precise the positive feedback the more powerful the impact will be.

Challenges are obviously trickier. As with positive feedback, you need to be as specific as possible. Instead of, "This bedroom is always a mess," say specifically, "We agreed to keep our clothes off of the floor and in the hamper. Could you please try and be more attentive to that?" Use their own desire to improve their personal habits to your advantage. "You know how you've talked about wanting to be more organized at work and in the office? Well starting in the bedroom might be a helpful way to get started." And be willing to support them and walk through the growth with them. "I'm being much more attentive to putting things away in the bathroom, so let's both be mindful of organization in each other's space, okay?" Also, just as you need to have prepared the concerns which you would like to talk about, have at least a potential answer to the challenge prepared. Don't be wedded to your solution, however, because your partner may have a creative idea which you haven't yet considered.

The most important thing about your critique is that it be based upon your previously agreed upon set of values and tasks. Part of the reason you need to be specific in your challenge is not simply so your spouse can see what upsets or annoys you but so that your spouse can see the way in which this prevents him from being all that he can and wants to be. This is why having those clear Job Descriptions set up ahead of time is so important, not so that you can hang something over their heads but so that you can hold up a mirror for them that they might see just where things stand.

## Good Coach/Bad Coach

While there is no one way to coach another person in virtue there are certainly better and worse ways of doing so. First of all, you must, even in the most trying of circumstances, provide *both* positive and redirecting feedback. Even if you're really angry at your spouse you need to find and name one positive thing about the person or nothing else you say will matter or be heard. In fact, if there weren't anything positive about them it's not clear why you'd be raising the issue with them at all!

Praise can be difficult both to give and to receive. Most people struggle with self-esteem and are their own worst critics, so it becomes easy to be dismissive of positive feedback and sensitive to negative feedback. Neither is really appropriate. It's often helpful to make a kind of rule that says that during the positive feedback sessions neither party is allowed to comment when receiving praise apart from, "Thanks" or "That means a lot." In this way, over time, your partner will come to see just how much you really do value them, their time, and their positive attributes.

Negative or redirecting feedback is oftentimes easier to take and harder to give. As with positive feedback, be clear, be direct, and reference the common set of expectations. Make clear especially how and why this particular behavior is troublesome for you and the ways in which you would like to see the behavior change. At the same time make clear your overall love and affection for your spouse and your willingness to help them change. Make offers, not ultimatums; encourage, don't accuse; challenge, don't blame. Show your willingness to help all along the way.

The most important thing, however, in giving both positive and redirecting feedback is making clear the context. In other words, your partner needs to know the context in which the problematic behavior occurred, or the new context in which the redirected behavior will take place. For example, say you hear something on the radio on the way home from work about keeping the romance alive in your marriage. Inspired, you stop by the florist and pick up a dozen roses. Your spouse, having not seen a show of affection like this in a long time, might say something like, "Ok, what did you do?" She lacks the context for the act of generosity. Likewise, she might make your favorite meal or dessert and you might wonder what she's going to ask for after dinner. Context is key for making behavior changes intelligible.

One way in which praising messages can be different than challenges, however, is that they need not be given in person. Praising messages via text, email, voicemail, cards hidden in suitcases, notes tucked into bathroom mirrors, or other surreptitious means can be sweet, affirming, and sexy. Use the tech to keep your romance alive. Challenges, on the other hand, should be delivered in person. First of all, it's easier to be misunderstood when you're not in person. Second, your partner deserves a chance to respond. Finally, it's going to become harder to work out a solution if you start out working separately than if you do so together.

## Redirect, Your Honor

The purpose of challenging your partner is not to point out their flaws but rather to redirect the behavior. For instance, if you and your partner are clearly experiencing tension over how often you have sex then your goal in pointing out that you feel pressured for sex too often mustn't be simply, "You're too needy and it annoys me." Undoubtedly your partner already knows that, probably feels guilty for it, and doesn't really know what to do about it. Your goal must be to help make them more aware of the problem and find a solution which not only makes the immediate problem (feeling pressured for sex) go away but at the same time redirects the energy from the behavior from something negative to something positive. Since the desire for sex is ultimately a desire for intimacy, encourage your partner to be more romantic: to buy flowers, make dinners, help clean the house, pitch in where he doesn't have to, or whatever special requests you might have, not simply so that he can be rewarded with sex but so that he can experience that desire being fulfilled in a radically different way. This will help him grow in virtue: not only in chastity and abstinence but in patience and goodwill.

One important difference between praising and challenging feedback is that while praising feedback should be more or less a monologue, not inviting lots of exchange, redirecting feedback should be more of a discussion, allowing for a fluid exchange of ideas and a clear articulation of emotions. There are a number of reasons for this. First, however upset you may have been at the individual behavior ahead of time, when you get to the meeting you need to be composed enough to articulate just how you have perceived the problematic behavior and why it bothers you, as well as open to listening to what your partner has to say. They may have vital information concerning the situation which you don't know yet and which could color the scenario very differently. They may be bothered by the behavior itself and have some helpful reflections on why this may or may not have happened; or they may have already come up with an action plan which could supplement or even replace whatever ideas you have come to the table with. Remember, it takes great humility to receive serious Virtue Coaching and show a willingness to change. Offer your spouse that same humility even as you challenge them to grow.

Before any attempt at challenge and redirection you should consider the following questions:

- Does your partner know the behavior does not meet your expectations? Do they know why?
- Does your partner know the value which is at play here and what you would want instead?
- Are there obstacles (of which you may not be aware) which are beyond your partner's control?
- Does your partner know how to do what you want them to do?

- Could your partner even do what you want them to if they wanted to? Can they do it alone or will they need your help or someone else's to accomplish it?

## Delivering the Message

Some behaviors don't quite fit either category; that is, some are neither the kind of habitual behaviors good to bring up in a regular feedback session nor the seriously problematic behaviors that need to be nipped in the bud fairly rapidly. Much of what you may struggle with about each other will be neither bad habits nor terrible decisions but something in between. In any case, the following principles can apply easily to all three situations:

**Set the Stage** – Depending upon the kind of concern, set a time for a meeting. It may fit well in your regular marital meeting schedule or it may be important to correct more quickly. One benefit to meeting sooner rather than later is that the event should still be fresh in your spouse's mind. It may not be if you wait two weeks to talk to them. Whatever you do, don't ambush your partner. Set up a time which works equally well for you both. Meet on neutral territory (if the kitchen is "yours" and the office is "theirs" then meet in the living room or on the deck instead).

**Share and Own Your Observations** – We only know what we see. You can make reasonable guesses about certain things but you shouldn't presume that you know the situation altogether until you've had a chance to talk about it. Simply describe the behavior as you observed or experienced it and articulate which shared values you feel have been violated. For example, "I saw you lose your temper with Alec three times in the last week over his math homework. I thought we agreed we weren't going to yell at the kids about school work."

**Explain Your Expectations** – Be clear with what you want your partner to do to both redirect or correct whatever has gone wrong in order to behave better in the future. "I would appreciate it if you could be more patient with Alec about his math."

**Listen To Your Spouse's Response** – This is very important. Your partner is likely to feel guilty and now put on the spot. Let them have their say and work through the feelings of anger, guilt, frustration, and incompetence. At the same time, be very fair and very serious; this is no place to try and justify legitimately bad behavior or explain it away. Be sure to consider legitimate circumstances which you don't know about that could color the picture very differently. If Alec had been misbehaving all day before you got home, for instance, then the loss of temper may have been more justifiable, or at least understandable, than it at first appeared to you. This is why it is important to ask clarifying questions, "Is there something that makes it difficult to be patient with him?"

**Negotiate a Solution** – This is where the teamwork really begins. Together with your partner work out a viable, realistic, and mutually agreed upon solution to the behavior which you are trying to redirect. It can be helpful at first to come up with a number of possible solutions. First of all, people are more likely to participate in solutions which they themselves help to create. If they cannot or will not offer their own input on the solutions then at least make your own suggestions about how the behavior might be redirected. "Should we trade off on homework duty the next few weeks?" Or maybe "Do you want to take the English and history homework and I take the math and science?" Remember, it's not about *who* is right but about *what* is right.

**Follow-up** – The best way to have an unsuccessful experience of feedback and challenge is to fail to follow-up on the redirected behavior. That's why it's important to put a date on the calendar in that very first meeting to talk about progress. The date may vary significantly depending upon the issue at hand. Sometimes it may simply be a matter of returning to the issue at your next meeting. Other times it may require follow-up the very next day. Be open with each other about what is possible and about possible timeframes. Don't expect mountains to move overnight and don't expect perfection right out of the box. The more deeply ingrained the behavior the longer it will take to correct. Old habits die hard and slow and it may take a number of sessions together before the undesirable behavior is successfully redirected.

Don't try to do everything on your own. You two are on a team but you're not playing alone. Don't be afraid to ask for help or find creative solutions which involve other people. You don't want to open up every skeleton-filled closet in your relationship but sometimes relying on the assistance of other people can go a long way. For example, if part of what is stressing out your husband and causing him to be impatient with your son doing his homework is the short window he has to get from work to school to pick him up and then from school to home to start dinner so that it's ready when you arrive, then maybe the solution is to have your neighbor who has a child in the same class pick your son up, too, and keep him until your husband gets home. On the other hand, if what's really eating your husband is a traumatic experience he had with math in grade school or the secret fear that he has of never being able to balance his checkbook then it's probably time to lovingly encourage him to get some outside help.

**Be Supportive** – The goal here is not to catch one another in mistakes. The whole enterprise of your marriage presumes that you have made mistakes and will continue to make mistakes, struggle with sin, and move towards holiness as we all do—more by fits and starts than by leaps and bounds. Every time you challenge your spouse with something, from the most minor personal habit to the most serious marital problem, they should know, above all else, that you love them, that you love them unconditionally, and that your goal here is your mutual perfection and growth in holiness, not a desire to hold something over against them.

Delivering a challenging message is never easy but there are things that we can do to make the experience less troublesome for all involved. In the end, the challenges which we experience in married life are only to make us better, stronger saints.

# A Touch of Business

In the business world nearly everyone hates performance feedback. Studies show time and again that both the employee and the supervisor, or whomever is assigned to give the feedback or critique, is uncomfortable with the process and dissatisfied with the result. Consequently, most feedback sessions fail to provide meaningful information to either party and so the action items which result are so vague as to be basically immeasurable. This is bad both for the individual and for the company. The individual never knows whether or not he's actually improving and the company is still left with the original concern intended to be addressed. Neither of these scenarios should sound very appealing for your marriage.

Despite the corporate baggage, giving and receiving concrete examples of what one does well and where one can improve can be extremely satisfying. This is because if a company's employees are performing well then the company is likely to be performing well too. Responsible corporations provide such feedback to their employees at least annually. This feedback should be based upon the employee's job description, perhaps with reference also to the values, standards, and objectives laid out in the company's Vision Statement and other documents. If a person were reviewed poorly, or even fired for failing to perform a job she was never asked to do, then there would be grounds for a wrongful termination complaint. In a similar way it would be unjust and unfair of you to hold your partner accountable for things which you had never discussed or never asked one another to do.

Therefore the key to good feedback begins with good expectations. If there are elements of your Vision Statement, Relationship Objectives, Job Descriptions, or assigned tasks which you feel are too vague or have inherent in them the possibility of serious misunderstanding then go back and revise them now. The purpose of designing those documents was not to fulfill an assignment but to provide you with a framework to better understand, maintain, and evaluate your relationship moving forward. Likewise, make sure the content of your Job Descriptions is clear. If at the start of your marriage you agree to take care of the bathrooms and your spouse agrees to tend to the kitchen then make sure that you are clear as to what your spouse's notion of a clean bathroom is and that they know what you expect in a well-organized kitchen. That isn't to say that you need to have every detail of your life together written down, but you want to make sure that you have a common starting point so that if conflicts do occur they can be negotiated in a way which is ultimately good for both of you.

Remember that the purpose of the feedback you offer one another in your marriage is to strengthen and sustain your relationship. The feedback should itself help to clarify expectations, both for you and for your partner as the relationship moves forward. When it works right, regular feedback sessions throughout the year, redirecting sessions when there are problems, and an annual or bi-annual assessment ensures that the day-to-day work of being in a relationship becomes an aid to developing an ever-deepening friendship founded on mutual trust, respect, intimacy, and forgiveness.

## A Word on Reconciliation

Reconciliation is essential to any authentically Christian relationship. We are bound to forgive one another, "as many as seventy times seven times," according to the Lord's command (Mt 18:22); which is to say, as often as we are asked. But this isn't just God replacing one set of commandments with another. Forgiveness is essential to the Christian life not simply because God has commanded it but because our relationships demand it. We aren't perfect people, and as such we screw up—most of us quite a bit—and need kind, generous, and understanding friends who are willing and able to see us through our mistakes, our errors, and our sins. The best of friends in the Christian life are the ones who love us in spite of our sins and help us work through them to become the person we were always meant to be.

This is especially true of Christian spouses. You've got to be willing to put up with a lot to be married; even the good ones still have a lot of brokenness to heal, a lot of guilt to overcome, a lot of sin to let go of, and a lot of room to grow. The uncomfortable truth about this arrangement, however, is that you have all of that too. One of the most powerful things about a Christian marriage is this sort of dynamic. By binding yourselves to one another you are binding yourself to a sinful human being, fully aware of the exposure that you're going to have to his or her sins for a lifetime, and yet confident that you will help each other grow to be something better by the end of it.

So let mutual forgiveness stand at the center of your relationship. This isn't just about "putting up" with another person whom you find mostly tiresome and annoying. Nor is it just about "learning to cope" with the mistake that you made once you realize that you really did have other choices. Instead, it's about fulfilling that promise of love and fidelity and learning, despite the weakness, sin, difficulty, and distress, to love them *more* than you did at first and to grow *more faithful* each and every day.

## Chapter Review

- What is virtue? What does it mean to say "Virtue lies in the mean/middle?" What sort of virtues do you think are especially important in married life?
- How can you help your spouse to become more virtuous? How can you best let them help you?
- What is an examination of conscience? How can that be helpful in the process of Reconciliation, both sacramentally and in your relationship?
- How can regular feedback provide a safe forum for you to help one another grow in virtue and holiness?

# CHAPTER 10:
# Family Time:
# Meetings and Retreats

*"Meetings are the new asceticism..."*

If you're like most people, then the last thing you need in the world is another meeting. In fact, one of the top complaints among employees and volunteers in almost every organization, from Microsoft and Google to your local little league and the global Catholic Church is, "Too many meetings!" In fact, employees often complain about being unable to accomplish their work because mandatory meetings take up so much time. Why, then, would we even suggest scheduling regular meetings as a couple?

First of all, companies and organizations do their employees a great deal of harm by holding a seemingly endless series of mostly unproductive meetings. Most of us have probably had the experience, even if only rarely, of attending a meeting that was run really well. You sit up and take note when you're at them because they are so unlike the regular sort of meetings you so often attend. And then an amazing thing happens: work *actually gets done.* So it is possible for meetings to accomplish something when organized well and properly run. Perhaps even more importantly, while frequent meetings that don't seem to get much done can be very tiresome, the alternative of institutionalizing an organized lack of communication is even more problematic. So any organization that wants to live, thrive, and survive needs to keep up and alive the regular flow of communication in order to move forward with new projects, generate new ideas, and attend to the necessities of running the operations. Your marriage is no different.

## Chapter Objectives

- Identify the importance of meetings and the characteristics of an effective one.
- Explain why spontaneous discussion is just not sufficient to deal with all aspects of a modern marriage.
- Come up with a sample agenda for a couple's meeting.
- Discuss the importance of retreats and how to make them fit into your schedules.
- Identify three ways in which you can consciously make time for each other.

# Let's Do Lunch

Most meetings fail because the moderator does one of two things: either the meeting is itself too informal a gathering and so it lacks structure and direction, or the meeting is well-organized and directed but so formalized and governed that the people gathered don't feel free to fully participate. Ironically, both are ultimately failures of communication, which is presumably the purpose for having the meeting to start with. For a meeting to be successful it needs to be sufficiently organized so that the purpose is clear, efficiently run so that the time is well spent, and have clear goals from the outset which are either attainable by the end of the meeting, or which can at least be measured in some objective way shortly thereafter.

Regular meetings are one of the best strategies for couples to employ to facilitate present conflict, avoid more serious difficulties in the future, and enhance overall happiness and satisfaction. Most of us can probably see the truth of this in the abstract but in part because of our own experiences of meetings, and also because most of our parents and grandparents didn't have regular "couple meetings"—at least so far as we knew at the time—we may wonder whether such an approach is even possible, let alone desirable. After all, most of us so busy right now that it's hard even to take care of ourselves and our needs. How can we possibly add a whole other set of meetings to make home look more like work? It's true enough that life is busy for all of us and that scheduling regular meetings is a meaningful sacrifice. But life has a way of happening anyway and you will surely be happier, both as a couple and as individuals, if you take the time to talk to each other on purpose. You will be reinforcing, both for yourself and for your spouse, the priority which you give to your relationship by setting aside time just to take care of each other and the relationship.

## The Spontaneous and the Purposeful

The most obvious critique of regularly scheduled couple's meetings is that you are already having them. Most mornings at breakfast you probably talk about your plans for the day and most evenings over supper you likely discuss what happened at work or at home. All of the times that you communicate with each other throughout the day—the conversations over meals, the series of texts while at the grocery store, the phone call in the middle of the day—all contribute to keeping the lines of communication open. Don't abandon these in favor of regularly scheduled meetings. Rather, supplement what you are already doing by being intentional about talking about your relationship, perhaps not least of all your preferred method of communication during the day!

There is simply no substitute for purposeful, structured, face-to-face meetings, especially if you or your spouse has to travel a great deal. Regularly scheduled, intentional meetings say to your spouse, "This is really still the most important thing to me," whether you've been married for six months, six years, or sixty years. Most couples do this best by setting up a regular schedule (like the first and third Tuesday, or the second and fourth Thursday of the month). Choose a time when you aren't both swamped with other things to do. Come as rested as you're able. If the nature of your work ensures that you are always tired after work, then consider having your meetings before you go in to start your shift. You will know which times, days, and major issues are appropriate to address in this context. What's important is that you set aside and dedicate time—real time—to talk about the minor and major issues in your relationship. You don't have to wonder what kind of a mood your spouse is in or how she'll react to particular questions or concerns, because both of you understand that this is the time to talk things through. This is the time to address shifts and adjustments in roles and responsibilities, the calendar for the coming weeks and possible conflicts, financial considerations, and issues surrounding the home and property. This purpose of the meetings is twofold: first, it provides a consistent and intentional time and space in which to discuss the "business matters" of your life together, something which oftentimes is neglected if not tended to directly; second, it provides a regular opportunity to discuss those things which you may be hesitant to bring up at the table, watching TV, or in the bedroom, because you know they make your spouse uncomfortable. This isn't the time for an all-out "spouse review"—we dealt with that in a previous chapter—but it is the time to initiate conversations about the day-to-day business of running your life together.

These gatherings should *never* be confused for "family meetings." Meeting together as a family is important and may well even be handled on the same night, but in family meetings the parents should feel comfortable primarily in their role as parent, whereas in the couple meeting they need to be thinking primarily in terms of husband and wife. It's not just that there are certain things which are inappropriate to discuss in front of the kids, though that's certainly true, but about the way in which you relate to each other. Your kids will appreciate it too, not only because they don't have to stick around for a meeting which only slightly involves them, but because they'll see the care which you both have for your relationship together. The best gift a father can give his sons and daughters is to be a good husband to their mom; likewise, the best gift a mom can give to her kids is to be a good wife. Regular meetings will not only help you to be good at your jobs but will in fact incline you towards excellence. Perhaps the best way to think of the difference between your couple meeting and your family meeting is in the difference between an "all staff" meeting at work and an "executive board" meeting. While *The Mission of Love*, which is your marriage, involves your kids, you two are really in the driver's seat together, and your kids will be looking to you for guidance.

## Guidelines for a Good Meeting

A great deal of work has been done in the corporate world to help managers run better meetings. Some of the same techniques which they employ will prove helpful for you as well.

**Agendas** – It may sound goofy and forced but having a written agenda is the first step to running a successful meeting. It doesn't have to be detailed but at least write down on a sheet of paper the two or three things you want to make sure you talk about this week. Both parties need to be able to contribute agenda items.

**Time** – Establish a definite time period for the meeting as a whole, and at least a general time period for the particular items under discussion. Don't make a habit of going over time. If an issue can be tabled until next time then usually that's the best thing to do, especially if you both have other things to do or places to be.

**Identify Outcomes** – Make clear for each agenda item, not simply what *you* would like to have happen but also what needs to be done on a minimal level to avoid some sort of bad consequence. For instance, if the interest rate changes on your student loans and you need to talk about it with your spouse, then put it on the agenda. Make clear that a decision needs to be made that evening for the next month's bill, though not necessarily a decision about the loan as a whole. Discussion may well take up the bulk of the meeting. If at the end of the meeting you still can't decide whether to pay the loan off outright or apply for a new payment plan, at least agree to make the first month's payment in order to avoid a penalty.

**Take Notes** – Keep track of at least the major things said and the actions decided upon.

**Stick to the Agenda** – Only allow items not on the agenda into the conversation if they have a real bearing on one of the agenda items. It can be easy to derail a difficult conversation with a pleasant distraction which both parties like better. Likewise, only add to the agenda if you genuinely need to and if both parties agree.

**Start and End on Time** – Since nothing seems to make people crazier than meetings that run late, do not introduce unnecessary tension into the meeting by raising the specter of a later meeting. If you both decide on twenty minutes or half an hour for your meeting, do not stay an hour. One or both of you will wind up resenting it and the decisions made in the meeting will likely turn out to be less than your best.

**No Interruptions** – This is really just common sense and respect but don't interrupt your partner. This time needs to be set aside purposefully. If that means scheduling the meeting around the baby's sleep schedule or Sarah's soccer game then that's what you need to do. Your kids shouldn't be able to walk into this meeting any more than they ought to be able to walk in on your lovemaking; this is an intimate exchange, even if of a very different kind, and you should keep it to yourselves. If you have other people living in your house, simply demand the time alone together. They need to either leave the house or be in some other room where they will not be distracting you.

**No Multitasking** – You wouldn't want your spouse to balance the checkbook or check the score of the game in the middle of an intimate encounter; likewise, be respectful of this time with your spouse. This is part of how you give yourselves to one another. Turn off the phones. Don't check your email. Tend to texts later. Just. Be. *Together.*

**Don't Insist** – Insisting on being in charge or right all of the time will only encourage unnecessary conflict. Trade the role of moderator and agenda setter each week. Allow the other to say their piece. Don't interrupt unnecessarily. Show your spouse how much you trust them.

**Be Open** – Part of the fun of being married is that you never really do know *all* that there is to know about your spouse. These meetings are for generating new ideas. Don't be dismissive. Let thoughts run for a bit. Try out new things in your head and let your spouse's insights influence you and vice-versa.

Here is a Sample Agenda:

# Agenda For Couples Meeting: Tuesday, October 8

Rachel's Items:

- Finances – Online bill payments for the cars; planning on selling the truck after first of the year, worth it in the meantime? How do we want to handle preschool tuition for Sarah? 5-7 minutes

- Babysitting – Regular daycare is still fine but Rachel is dissatisfied with the neighbor girl they've been using on the weekends. Ask around at Church on Sunday? 2-5 minutes

- Special Events – How do we handle Halloween? Sarah's birthday is the following week? Combine the two or keep them separate? If one of us takes her trick-or-treating who stays at home? 8-10 minutes

- Vacation Planning – What are the latest figures on a cabin for a week? Is it worth tent-camping with a four year old? 5 minutes

- Gifts – Sarah's birthday: something big or hold off till Christmas? Also, Mom's birthday is the first week of November. Ideas? 3-5 minutes

Kyle's Items:

- Finances – Getting ready to sell the truck, ideas on next vehicle? What about selling his classical guitar? Could help with tuition. 5 minutes

- Lawn and Maintenance – Leaves starting to fall: mulch, compost, or remove? 2-3 minutes

- Car Maintenance – Acura needs oil, fluids, and filters changed before winter; new tires for season on the car, wait on the pickup? 5 minutes

- House Projects – Priced for a shower stall in basement bathroom. Is it worth it? Also, upstairs toilet still acting up. Time to call the plumber? 5 minutes

- Business Trip – Kyle's sister has volunteered to come and stay to help take care of Sarah while Rachel is away on business. Any specifics? 2-3 minutes

- Church – Feels rushed on Sunday morning. Conversation about a later Mass? 3-5 minutes

In order to make sure that the meeting runs efficiently it can be helpful at the start to combine discussion items. For instance, in the example above, both Kyle and Rachel feel the need to talk about the impending sale of their pickup. Rather than go through all of Rachel's items and then all of Kyle's, they should combine their discussion of finances and car maintenance so that the conversation isn't started, stopped, and then started again.

Another important thing to do is to periodically take a few minutes and evaluate the effectiveness of the meeting itself. This will be more important earlier on in the relationship than later but every third or fourth time it would be worth asking your spouse: Is this working for you? How can we spend our time better? Is there a more efficient, fair, or reasonable way to discuss these things? The temptation early on will be to abandon the meetings altogether, to talk about the cars on Saturday morning when he goes to work on the car, or to talk about tuition when she goes to write the check. DO NOT GIVE IN TO THIS TEMPTATION!

The trouble is that if you wait until Saturday morning or Sunday afternoons when he usually works on the cars or the lawn to talk about them, the conversation will be unplanned, will likely take longer, may never result in any kind of conclusion, and will have eaten into his time to actually work on the cars. Likewise, if the tuition conversation doesn't happen until she's writing the check the week that it is due, and he volunteers to sell his guitar, then they might do so rashly, whereas if they plan a conversation about it she will have the opportunity to suggest alternatives. These meetings are about *opportunity*. They give your spouse the opportunity to be your spouse, to hear your concerns and offer insights which you might not have yourself, and to accomplish something which you couldn't do on your own

.

## Keep It Simple

The key to a successful couple meeting is to keep it as simple as possible. This is not the time to discuss the complexities of the national debt or the housing market. Don't let yourselves get distracted by things only tangentially related to the issues at hand. Don't mix up agenda items or go out of order unless both partners agree to. And *don't ever* use these regular business meetings as an occasion to vent at your partner or even constructively review their job performance, emotional paycheck, or lack of benefits. That will destroy the trust which you both need to have in order for these meetings to work effectively, plus will work *against* your ability to have those important conversations in the appropriate ways and at the appropriate times.

Most businesses find that short but frequent staff meetings are more productive than meeting only rarely but for longer periods of time. Having a bi-weekly couples meeting of 20-30 minutes will be more productive than an hourly meeting once a month, not least of all because there will be less to discuss and the items should be in more manageable, bite-sized chunks. Also, complexity can be disruptive. Have your agenda items ready the night before and give them to your spouse by the morning of the meeting. That way whomever is moderating that night can combine those topics which should be put together for clarity's sake and may even see that something can be tabled for the next meeting. Sometimes this is a practical decision but other times it can be an issue of sensitivity. Let's say that the three main things which you need to discuss on a given night are your daughter's declining grades, lawn care for the summer, and paying off the balance on a student loan. Your daughter's grades are likely to be an emotional issue for you both. The student loan is probably an issue which is time sensitive. So unless something needs to be done or decided concerning the lawn *today*, or at least in the next two weeks, common sense says to table the lawn care conversation and tackle the issues which need to be handled more immediately.

Another technique consists in arranging the schedule of a meeting to maximize the emotional effects of the meeting itself. For example, some weeks it may be best to start with the fun, simple, and easier issues before taking up the more challenging discussion items. At other times it may be best to do the opposite: wrestle the elephant in the room first but make sure you have a "carrot" for yourselves at the end of the meeting to motivate you through it. Or, on occasion (though this should be *very* occasional), consider calling a special meeting for a special topic. In the last example a child's grades were falling. This may be a good time to have a special meeting, probably immediately before or after having a meeting together as a family with the child in question. Also, consider beforehand what type of meeting this is. Will it be primarily about discussion, making decisions, problem-solving together, or just general information sharing, coordinating schedules, and monthly planning? The character of the meeting, determined by the agenda items, will largely shape what type of meeting it is and so may affect where, when, and how you choose to have it.

Finally, a sure-fire way to start the meeting off right, especially if any of the issues you have to discuss are likely to be difficult, is to start with a prayer. This may be difficult at first, especially if you haven't really developed a comfort in praying with each other yet. Simply pause for a moment and then ask God to bless your time together, to be present among you as you tend to important things, to give you the wisdom to make good decisions together, the openness to hear new and good ideas from one another and to be changed by one another, and the insight to see God's action in the other person. Ending the meeting with a prayer thanking God for the time together is a good thing too, as is taking a few moments to affirm the other in their contributions to the meeting and the good order of your life together. Be respectful of differences in each other's beliefs and prayer styles (i.e., if one of you is not Catholic do not start off with a Hail Mary), and then be genuinely attentive to the ways in which God may be moving you through the course of the meeting.

## Retreat, Recharge, Renew

"Retreat" in a church context is something of a loaded word these days. Up until the 1950s, going on "retreat" was something only priests and nuns did, usually for a week once a year at a very strict and silent monastery. In the 1950s, priests started to include lay people on their retreats, sometimes silent, and sometimes with talks throughout the day. In the 60s, this morphed into a more social model of retreat where a group of people would go away for a weekend or so for prayer, fellowship, and talks meant to encourage one another in the spiritual life. These retreats were often themed and became associated with movements like Cursillo, TEC, and Lifeteen. Eventually retreats specifically for couples were devised, things like Marriage Encounter, Engaged Encounter, and Retrouvaille. You may or may not be familiar with any of these, or you may have been required by your pastor or the diocese to take advantage of one of these in the course of your marriage preparation. Today all of these models still exist: priests and religious are still required to go "on retreat" for a week each year, and all sorts of specialized retreats of varying length exist for virtually every kind of religious group imaginable.

Businesses hold corporate retreats too, often for executives to set aside time outside of the office or usual place of work to go away together, look at long-range planning, set up new objectives for the organization, evaluate the current situation, and generate new ideas. Whatever the content of a business retreat, it usually focuses on the higher-level company issues rather than the day-to-day business usually covered in a staff meeting.

Whether you have ever been on a retreat before or not, taking time away on purpose to recharge yourselves and renew your relationship is absolutely essential. It used to be that "Priests went on retreat; people went on vacation," but now we all have the opportunity, and maybe even the obligation, to set aside time to work especially on what's most important to us. The reason the Church requires priests and religious to go on retreat is because the life of a priest can be very active: running a parish, administering sacraments, visiting the sick, tending to the poor, running a school; in the midst of all of this even he can lose track of his own vocation—that whole complex of prayer and study and good works and relationships that make up his own way to God. The same is true for married couples: the house, the bills, the kids, the in-laws, work, school, friends, social obligations, hobbies, outside interests, and even church can all get in the way or distract us from *The Mission of Love*—our way to God through our spouse. The reason the Church calls marriage a sacrament is because your spouse is the very particular way that God is trying to save you; your last, best chance of heaven is the person you lie down next to every night. What could be more important than caring for that?

So periodically, at least once or twice a year, you need to take time apart. Ideally this should happen outside of your house, apartment, or condo. The kids can't be involved. You shouldn't be readily available to family or friends. This is for you and your spouse. It's part of the reason you got married, and you two won't be able to fulfill the other reasons you got married (service of God and neighbor, sign of Christ's love to the world, etc.) if you don't first take care of your relationship together. You can be creative with how you do it. Sometimes you'll see specials for a hotel or spa, or maybe you're into camping, and the wilderness is a better place for you both to go away for a while. If you're already going on vacation, then maybe simply setting aside a day or two in the midst of that time away would be best (send the kids to the children's camp for the day or meet up with old friends and allow the kids to play together). Sometimes necessity (financial, health, or otherwise) demands that the retreat be "at home" but even then your regular living space should somehow be transformed for the period involved. Turn off your phones, computers, and unplug the modem for the day. Agree ahead of time on how to handle food. This would be a good time to switch up who usually does the cooking and the clean-up, or maybe agree on doing it together in a way different than the usual. Change the sheets and linens. Bring out your best tableware. However you can, mark this time, this day, as separate, different, even *holy*.

What do you do during this time? As with your regular meetings you will need an agenda, though you might not want to stick to time restrictions in the same way. What you really need are your Vision Statement and Relationship Objectives, your marital Brand, your Job

Descriptions, the Compensation and Benefits package and motivator lists, Virtue Coaching feedback and, most especially, each other. This is a time to quietly, reflectively, prayerfully sit back and take stock of things. See what's working well and what isn't, and creatively devise new ways to do things better.

The agenda itself should consist of three or four large blocks of time (at least an hour each) during which you can cover the following:

- Revisit, re-evaluate, or re-adopt your Vision Statement and Relationship Objectives. Are you still both on the same page? What adjustments might be necessary? A helpful exercise during this session might be to name two or three moments over the course of the last year when you were very conscious of fulfilling your Vision together.

- Get an update on the family's overall financial picture. This is especially important if one or the other of you is the one to primarily deal with the family finances. Don't sugarcoat the truth with each other. If things are tough and you need to start cutting back then talk openly and honestly about the things which you reasonably can do without. If things are good and there is some extra cash, talk about how to spend, save, or invest that money.

- Discuss long-term issues which affect your life together. How is your parents' health? What are the family's plans once they need more care? Are you comfortable with that? What about your own health and that of your spouse? Is it time to have another child? Is it time to refrain from having another child?

The most important part of the retreat time is the formal "performance feedback meeting" discussed in an earlier chapter. You may well have these outside of the retreat setting but you shouldn't really let one of these retreat days go by without each offering one. This may involve a discussion of the Relationship Covenant, your Job Descriptions, the Compensation and Benefits package, and the overall way in which your spouse is fulfilling their obligations, not only to you but to God and to *The Mission of Love*. There should be no surprises here because you will have both been praising, challenging, and redirecting one another throughout the year. This is surely a time to offer redirection feedback to one another, but what is needed to discuss these challenges is an atmosphere of love and affirmation. "I'm still here because I want to be," you're saying to your spouse, "and I want to be here because I still believe in us and what we have to offer the world."

The retreat will involve some hard internal and external work but it should also be fun. In between "workshop" sessions, recreate together: hang out at the pool, snorkel, hike, golf, get a couples' massage, read to each other, make music together, cook for each other and eat with each other—*play together*. And don't feel guilty at all, especially if you have kids. This is part of being a good parent. It isn't indulgent, it's about self-care. If you're having a little trouble getting your minds around just what one of these weekends might look like then you might want to try a group weekend to start. Check with your local parish, they should have information on the next diocesan-wide event. These can give you a good sort of "jump start" to begin planning weekends of your own.

Find some way to incorporate prayer into the mix as well. Certainly beginning and ending each of the sessions, especially the feedback sessions, would be important. More than that, though, take time to be together in silence. Watch a sunset together and marvel at God's beauty. Pray over your favorite bits of Scripture together. As you read over your Vision Statement go back to your wedding vows themselves: pray over them and talk about them, about how they're still your ideal and how you match up to them and how sometimes you don't. Attend Mass at a nearby parish if you are able or go to an hour of Eucharistic Adoration together (this is often a good idea even the week before, to get both of you into the mood of the retreat). Go to confession together and when your spouse is in with the priest spend your time in the church on your knees praying especially for them and their relationship with God. Put yourself in God's Presence and let Him be present to you.

Finally, this time of retreat is a most appropriate time for lovemaking as a couple. A whole host of other things play into this as well: health, emotional state, reproductive concerns, and all the rest; but it should be sort of obvious that the days during which you are most intentionally considering your life together are the days during which you should be recommitting yourselves to one another soul *and* body. The Church teaches that every time a married couple makes love they are engaging in a sacramental act, sealing again the covenant they made that day at the altar. It may not always feel like it, and it might well not feel like it on the retreat, but healthy, holy sex is one of the best ways to ensure the health and stability of your relationship.

## Conclusion

You should come back from your retreat refreshed in body and in spirit. This time should give you the chance to regain perspective and set out again for the goals you established so long ago. Each one won't be perfect, but if you can enter into the time openly and honestly, doing your best to be present to one another and to the Holy Spirit, then your marriage will only be stronger and you will be better spouses for each other than you were before.

### Chapter Review

- Why are meetings important? Provide an example of how a "spontaneous meeting" or regular conversation did not work in your regular life.
- Identify days/times that would be good for regular meetings.
- List at least five characteristics of good couple meetings.
- Discuss the possibility of adding a "retreat day" to your vacation or setting time aside before or after for a retreat.
- Talk about why retreats are important to you and how to fit them into your busy schedules.

# CHAPTER 11:
## Prayer: the Final Frontier

This may be the last chapter of the book but it stands as the very foundation of the whole *Mission of Love*. By now you have surely seen that your love has a purpose, and that your greatest joy and fulfillment in life will come when that purpose, that goal, that mission is finally accomplished. But the *Mission of Love* is no invention of your own imagination, no mere product of your minds, alone or together. Rather, it is a calling, a high calling, a divine vocation, given to you by the very God who made you.

### Chapter Objectives

- To be able to explain why prayer is important generally, and why it is so vital in the life of a couple.
- To summarize the main reasons people give for finding prayer difficult, both alone and together, and to provide some basic responses.
- To better understand the Church's liturgical and devotional life and how that can enrich your life as a couple and as a family.
- To articulate the formative power of liturgy and devotions in the life of a family.

## Seeing Things New

Suppose a kindergarten teacher were to ask her students to draw anything they liked on a piece of paper. They would happily oblige and draw any number of things: some simple, some abstract, perhaps even some very strange. If the teacher were to hang these pictures in the hall for everyone to see, they would likely attract snickers from the older students because, well let's face it, they're not really going to be that good. But suppose the parents of these children were to walk down those halls and see their child's picture. To them it would be the most beautiful thing in the world, and it has nothing to do with any objective artistic standards. It's not that they will fail to see all the imperfections, like the lack of proportion or coloring outside the lines, but the simple fact for them remains: the parents know where the picture came from. These parents are so deeply in love with their children that their creations and expressions arouse a sincere and lasting joy in their hearts. Their child's art is always the best, or at least they always love it better, because it is *their child's*.

When you behold your spouse, something of the same thing happens. He or she is a gift far more beautiful, and they speak even more eloquently of the One who made them. You see, the more we fall in love with the Creator, the more we fall in love with the one He created for us. It's not that our appreciation will blind us to their imperfections but rather that it opens our eyes to a more profound view, a God's-eye view, of the greater beauty inherent in them as one made in the image and likeness of God.

This is the significance of prayer. Prayer is relationship. It's not simply a means of communication, or a specialized way of speaking. Prayer is nothing else than the ongoing relationship which one has with God. In the Catholic tradition there are myriad types of prayer, so many that at times it can seem overwhelming. But this should not surprise us. Just as there are a seemingly infinite variety of people, so there are a seemingly infinite variety of ways for those people to relate to God. But the heart of all authentic Christian prayer is *communion* with God, a constant and ever-deepening falling in love with our Creator. This relationship deepens our bond with Him and opens our hearts and minds to His ever present will, especially as revealed in those whom He has given us to love here on earth.

## It Starts At Home

"Lord, let me know myself," St. Augustine used to say. He understood that at the heart of all prayer was a profound self-knowledge. St. Catherine of Siena used to talk about the "cell of self-knowledge," or we might say, the study of self-reflection. It's not that in prayer we are simply talking to ourselves but that communication with God necessarily involves us on every level—especially those most intimate and interior levels where our true selves live and where most of us seldom visit.

The word communication is derived from the Latin word *communio* meaning "mutual participation." Rightly understood, communication is not merely about talking and listening, but entering into and having a shared experience with another. Prayer, as communication with our Lord, then, is not simply a matter of talking or, as both Paul and our Lord rebuke in Scripture, rattling off words in the hopes that someone might hear us. Rather, it is a radical opening of oneself up to an encounter with the very source of Life and of Love. And, like any form of communication, this will differ according to each individual. Our Lord has a *personal relationship* with each and every one of us and does not simply come to us in a generic sense. God is not an abstraction but a person, a communion of persons, which is why the Blessed Trinity stands as the central mystery of our faith. At the very heart of God there exists a communion of persons—a common shared experience. God knows what it's like to relate to us as an individual. He speaks to us as He knows us and as He loves us, as unique, unrepeatable, irreplaceable individuals. In developing a prayer life it will be necessary to "know thyself," to become aware of one's own innate temperament, and to come to grips with one's own personal baggage.

Temperaments and personalities are critically important in the beginning. For example, as an extravert, an open recitation of the rosary with others close to you might be a very enriching encounter. However, as an introvert, you may prefer the silent recitation of the rosary, alone in stillness, with the words serving as a centering tool that immerses you into meditation on each one of its Mysteries. Neither of these is right or wrong, good or bad. Much as with growing up, one simply needs to learn one's own needs and wants, attitudes and personality quirks, and then attend to them appropriately.

This is not an exact science but think of the times you felt most fulfilled and loved in your own relationship with your spouse. Use these as a guide. There is a reason we respond the way we do in relationship and our relationship with God will be no different. The wonderful thing about grace is that it cannot be contained. As you foster a healthy prayer life, the outpouring of grace will not only lead to your growth and enrichment but, like a warm fire during a cold winter night, its comforting effects will be felt by those around you too, most especially your spouse and children.

As with all things, we cannot be content simply with our own preferences. First, as human beings, if we satisfy ourselves simply with that which is pleasing to us now then we miss out on a whole variety of experience. Second, and more importantly, as members of the Church we have an obligation to each other. That's why we have to learn about and be present to the prayer life of other members of Christ's Body. The Church assures that in a special way through the weekly celebration of the Eucharist but also in a more day-to-day way through the lives of prayer of the other members of our family. This is especially true of our spouses.

## We Go Together

Most couples do not pray together, which is probably one key reason so many marriages fail. That doesn't mean that if you aren't presently praying together that your marriage is doomed, or that if you don't turn your house into a mini-monastery that divorce is always looming around the corner, but the old saying is as true for a family of two as it is for a family of fifteen: "The family who prays together, stays together."

If you do not currently pray together as a couple, consider yourself in the majority. Surveys on the subject show time and again that the main reason couples don't prayer together is it's just too intimate. This is really significant. First, the uncomfortable feelings that can result from the prospect are precisely why you must pray together as a couple. These feelings are rooted in the fact that religion is not simply a ritual but speaks to our inmost being: what we believe is our purpose, how we define right and wrong, and even the nature of our very existence. There is, perhaps, nothing more intimate about ourselves to be shared with another. No wonder we're reluctant to do so. No marriage has ever succeeded, however, with only an exterior facade or a series of ritual promises. In this sacrament you become "one flesh" in spirit and in truth; this requires a complete gift of yourself to the other—not just a part of yourself but the whole shebang.

134

Marriage is a sacrament. Sacraments make tangible and accessible the intangible and supernatural. God pours out His strength and sanctifying grace to us in ways that we can handle it. Think, for instance, of the Eucharist. Even after it has been consecrated it still looks, smells, tastes, and feels like ordinary bread but something—the most important thing, in fact—has been changed. What looks like bread has become Body; what tastes like wine has become Blood. Marriage, as a sacrament, is no different. What continues to look like two distinct lives and ways of being in the world has been radically merged; two have become one, even if they still appear to be two. And just as with the Eucharist the presence of Christ remains so long as what appears to be bread remains, so also in marriage so long as what appears to be two remain they are in fact one. The sacrament of Holy Matrimony is not a one-shot ceremony on a Saturday afternoon, it's the whole of your married life together. This means whatever you do with and for one another has been transformed by God, infused with grace, and made into a "sacramental," a living channel of God's own light and life. When you live out the promises you made on your wedding day, you make tangible the supernatural, you make present the eternal, you embody the "one flesh" union which came into being when you first professed your vows—and you renew it together again and again and again.

## Feeling Your Way Along

The point is that praying together as a couple is likely the most intimate thing you will ever do together. It can be light years more intimate than sex, which is the reason that so many couples, married and unmarried, find it easier to sleep together than to pray together. But done rightly, it will infuse and affect and transform every aspect of your relationship— including sex. Your home life will be better, your emotional life will be more livable, your financial situation will be more sustainable, and yes, even the sex will get better, not because prayer magically changes everything or because God only blesses those who talk to him a lot, but because by showing your heart to your spouse, by giving them something else which only God ever gets to see, they'll understand you better and love you more. And you'll do the same for them.

Of course, the other reason for not praying together also needs to be addressed: We don't know how. Now it's funny, when you ask couples about this relative to the sex question they'll often say something like, "Well, sex we just kind of figured out together (or with someone else a whole lot earlier) but nobody ever really taught us to pray together." If you feel like this you are not alone. It's entirely possible to have gone the whole way through Catholic school and not really have a great sense of how to pray together. And the connection to sex isn't crazy: this is something that you're going to have to learn together, and there will probably be a lot of fumbling around to start, with uncomfortable silences and starting-and-stopping and all the rest. But in the end you'll settle into a pattern, a pattern which should periodically be shaken up but which proves good, holy, and healthy for the two of you.

Praying together can be as simple or involved as you both want: from attending some liturgical service together (Mass, Adoration, the Divine Office, etc.), to saying the rosary while you take your morning walk, to simply holding each other when you first wake up and thanking God for the gift of the other, whether aloud or in silence. Given that you and your spouse complement each other with both differences and similarities it is likely that some kinds of prayer will be good for you both, some will nourish one, and some will nourish the other. Remember that your partner has real spiritual needs and that you need to be attentive to them. What may be super-important for you might be boring as all get-out for your spouse but you need to engage it as often as you can for their sake, and what's more, you even need to learn to love it, if for no other reason than for the peace and joy it brings them. Of course there are certain things, like weekly Mass, that you need to be attentive to whether you seem to be "getting a lot out of it" or not, because the Church asks it of all of us, and because it's how we stay connected with the wider Christian community.

Sheer gratitude for your life together, if nothing else, should be a sufficient motivator for engaging this part of your life together. You don't thank God for a lifetime with your spouse in the way you thank someone for holding the door or passing the salt. God has literally given you everything, and in your spouse He's given you the best thing you've got. And what you'll learn, as you engage and cultivate this gratitude together, is that you become more and more grateful to and appreciative of your spouse as well.

## Family Ties

Prayer together as a family is important not only as a bonding exercise for the couple but because it reinforces and communicates *The Mission of Love* in the sacrament. You pray together each day for the same reason the monks in the monastery and the priests in the Church do—because prayer is what Christians do, and because when Christians are together they pray together. As we have pointed out in earlier chapters, your family is a "domestic church," the most vital cell of society and of the Church. Just as every parish has a schedule of services and every religious house lives by a certain rule of life, so also your homes should be marked by a regular pattern of prayer which punctuates the day and gives meaning to work, recreation, and all the rest. Not only is the mission you received in the sacrament of Matrimony meant to lead to your ultimate joy and fulfillment, but the way that you live this mission out will be the primary way that you pass the Faith on to your kids and teach them the values that are most important to you. Through your regular prayer as a family you will teach your children about their inherent dignity and the high calling of their own Christian vocation, about the worth of life and of love, and about their place in the Church and in the world.

## Daily Rituals

One of the greatest mysteries for the human mind to ponder is the relationship between God and time. God is infinite and eternal, and yet finite and temporal in the person of Jesus Christ on earth. Jesus Christ was begotten by the Father before all ages and has always existed. In fact, Jesus is the only person that can say His existence preceded His birth. Time also has a very important role to play in our salvation as well. Jesus Christ and the atonement for our sins were not given to us the moment Adam and Eve had sinned—it took *time*. It took several millennia to prepare the way for Christ and two millennia have transpired since this redemptive act as we inch closer to the Second Coming and the ultimate completion of God's plan.

> The economy of salvation is at work within the framework of time but since its fulfillment in the Passover of Jesus and the outpouring of the Holy Spirit, the culmination of history is anticipated "as a foretaste," and the kingdom of God enters into our time (*CCC* 1168).

So, the bad news is that as mortal beings on this earth we are bound by time. The good news is that time is not a hindrance to proper worship and adoration of God—it is ordained by Him and, as in all of God's creation, He is to be glorified in it and through it.

In the universal Church, the liturgical seasons exist for this very reason. They are not a celebration of time itself but a participation in the eternal, Paschal sacrifice celebrated within time. Through the way that we pray in the different seasons and the mysteries we reflect on at particular times, we gain a deeper understanding of the whole of Christ's redemptive act and our worship of Christ in the Holy Sacrifice of the Mass. The Mass is, in itself, always perfect and complete but by celebrating it in different ways and at different times, the fullness of meaning contained in the Mass becomes clearer. What's more, the liturgical seasons foster a unity among the Mystical Body of Christ's faithful here on earth as in the Church throughout the world we participate in the same seasons and traditions.

What in the world does any of this have to do with being married? Again, as a married couple you are the domestic church, the cell which forms that Mystical Body of Christ. Just as the universal Church celebrates the many liturgical seasons throughout the year, it is important that you, as a domestic church, participate in these seasons as well. It is through you that your children will come to understand the deeper mysteries of their larger family, the Church here on earth and in heaven. And while it is important to participate in some of the more general customs of the secular community, it is absolutely imperative that in your celebration your focus remains on the spiritual and liturgical aspects—the spiritual reasons for the seasons. Walmart might put up Christmas decorations before Halloween but we Christians celebrate in seasons, and the prep-time offered in Advent makes for a much more meaningful Christmas than *Frosty the Snowman* on Thanksgiving Day.

Our worldview and value system come primarily from our family life, not only by what our parents say and teach but by the feasts we keep and the fasts we observe, by the parties we have and the celebrations we skip. In order to teach our children what is most important we must put our focus on what the Church holds up for us in each particular season or celebration. Of course, the goal is not just to know all sorts of Catholic trivia but rather to live deeply within the tradition so that, over time, the fullness of meaning will become more and more clear to each member of the family, and the experience of coming to know this together spiritually will bond that family more closely forever. This is what connects us not only to one another but to the larger Catholic community as well. We as a family take much of what identifies us from the Church, so we are connected as Catholics both within our domestic church and with others in the wider community.

There are loads of examples for each season and the various feasts. Books have been written about it and whole websites are dedicated to it. Each family is invited to draw richly from the deep well of resources which is the Church's tradition. But in a secular society which seems to draw further and further away from its Christian roots, sometimes making distinctions is important. Setting up an Advent Wreath and lighting the candles at dinner is a good way to remind everyone that even though Christmas lights might already be up and the parties already started, we are still waiting. Likewise, the community Easter Egg Hunt might happen the Saturday before Palm Sunday but setting the goodies aside until Easter morning is a good way to help the children (and adults) keep the fast and remember the feast. Another great practice is to bring items from our daily life to the priests of the Church to have them blessed. If your highschooler gets a new laptop or tablet for Christmas, for instance, have them bring it with them to Mass on Sunday and ask Father to bless it after Mass. This helps to make holy things which we might otherwise think of as simply secular.

There's nothing which touches on our life together as Christians which can't rightly be blessed. Together you as a family will come up with your own cycle of feasting and fasting, and your own particular traditions. Just be sure you take the traditions of the wider Church as your guide.

## Liturgical Prayer and Devotions

Because the domestic church participates in the wider life of the universal Church your lives of prayer should reflect that of the Church universal. This means, at a minimum, getting to Mass on Sunday. Of course that can be hard, and we've all had times where we fall short, but this isn't about some silly rule or abstract ideal. Sunday Mass is important for the same reason Sunday dinner is important; at least once a week we need to be fed, *really fed*, both body and soul. And we can't claim to continue to be part of a family that we never see. Sometimes, if we're able, we might be able to get to Mass more often—to get fed more often—and to connect more closely and more frequently with that family.

But the Church's prayer is more than Mass. There are also the gifts of the sacraments. Most parishes have a communal Reconciliation Service during Advent and Lent but your parish priest probably also hears confessions on Saturday, and maybe during the week before daily Mass. Go to confession as a family and bring your kids along. Your spouse can watch them while you're in with Father and vice-versa. But if your kids see you going to Reconciliation and taking seriously your own struggle with sin, then they will be more likely not only to be better behaved but to appreciate just how much the Faith means to you. Take your kids to weddings (provided there isn't one of those silly "No kids allowed" provisos on the invite). Let them see what it means to get married. Likewise, keep an eye on the parish bulletin or diocesan newspaper. When the kids are old enough, bring them to an ordination so that they can see how priests and deacons are made. Bring them to family baptisms and the parish confirmation. And if Grandma or Grandpa needs anointing, then arrange with the priest so that the kids can see that too. Familiarity here will not bring contempt, but appreciation and comfort.

The Church in recent years has also called for the laity—that's you—to participate more in the Divine Office. You know that little red or black book Father carries around with him? Well, it's a kind of manual of prayers for different times of the day, called either the Divine Office (because it's the work God has given us to do), or the Liturgy of the Hours (because there are set prayers for different times of the day). It's a very ancient prayer, inspired by the prayer of the Jews in the Temple, which is composed mostly of the psalms but also with readings, prayers, and hymns for the particular hours of the day. It's a way for the Church to sanctify the whole day and to together keep Paul's admonition to "Pray without ceasing." Now some try to do this by buying sets of books and attempting the whole thing at home, and maybe if you have especially well-behaved kids you can do that, but most of us have to make adjustments. The pattern, though, of praying in the morning, in the evening, and at night is good for all of us to follow. Night Prayer, especially, is short and pretty easy. It's composed of a hymn, a psalm or two, a short reading, a song from the gospel, a prayer, and then a very special hymn to Mary (a kind of lullaby for the Church). There are also different worship aids developed especially for lay people on the move which are inspired by the Liturgy of the Hours and even include all or part of them. These also often include the readings of the day from Mass, which can be really helpful to read over, even if you can't get to Mass.

## Hopelessly Devoted

And then there's the whole devotional life of the Church. These are prayers which, while not part of the Church's official liturgy, are meant to draw our hearts and minds closer to the celebration of it. A great example is the rosary. We've all seen rosaries, and probably most of us learned to say the rosary at least in Catholic grade school or CCD. The rosary is an especially good prayer for families because everyone, from the child just old enough to talk to the elderly person who may even have lost the ability to speak, can follow along. All you have to do is be able to thumb the beads and say, at least quietly to yourself, the Our Father, the Hail Mary, and the Glory Be. It was developed as a prayer for illiterate peasants who couldn't follow along with the psalms since they were sung in Latin, but it has become over the centuries the most popular devotion in the whole history of the Church. Everyone, from the poorest peasant to the most sophisticated philosopher, knows it and uses it. It's a good thing to teach your kids early on, so that they have it as a tool when things get tough.

But rosaries aren't the only devotion at work in the Church. In fact, many devotions are rooted directly in liturgical seasons or feasts. Advent wreaths and trees, Lenten fasts, May Crowning, cemetery visits for All Souls' Day, weaving palms, thrush crosses for St. Brigid, blessing candles for the Feast of the Presentation, blessing throats on St. Blaise Day, the list could go on and on. Ethnic practices connected to particular feasts can be important, and helping your kids to celebrate their *Onomastico*, or Saint's Day, can also be lots of fun. This helps to situate your kids within the context of Church history; it helps to give them personal and spiritual roots, and gives them both a model to follow and an example to aspire to.

The point of the Church's devotional practices is not to load up more things for you and your family to do, or suck up even more time with church stuff, or turn your house into a shrine to Saint-What's-Her-Name and celebrate every obscure feast. Rather, the point is to help you place faith at the center of your family life, not as a pious add-on nor as some kind of background music that you only notice at Christmas and Easter, but as the vital and defining force which gives spiritual shape, texture, and depth. That's the reason some of the things that seem so old-fashioned like "Consecrating" your family to the Blessed Virgin Mary or "Enthroning" the Sacred Heart in your family home are so important—they don't make us more religious, they help us stay more consistent.

## Conclusion

If you follow the analogy of the Church as a family, then liturgies are something like family dinners and devotions are like the party games or annual outings. To borrow a basically secular example, if we say that Thanksgiving is a really formative and important holiday for us as a family, that it forms us in gratitude and helps us to be more loving and generous people, we primarily think of the family dinner itself. But we also mean the whole series of events that lead up to and follow from it: helping cook the night before, watching or playing football afterwards, cards and turkey sandwiches on Thanksgiving night, and even getting up early to shop on Black Friday. And just as in our families some devotions are for everyone (e.g. *everybody* watches *It's the Great Pumpkin, Charlie Brown* on Halloween), some are particular to certain members (you and three of your cousins always go to the movies the day after Christmas while your spouses are returning Christmas presents). The goal is to see in the Church the same kind of variety of practice and also the way in which it forms us, and the degree to which we let ourselves be formed by it.

One final word: if praying anything apart from grace before meals together as a couple seems really intimidating right now, then "Enthroning the Sacred Heart in Your Home," or attending the Liturgy of the Hours three parishes over probably seems impossible, and that's okay. Nobody's asking you to go from zero to sixty in the spiritual life all at once. You've got a lifetime together to explore your faith but you'll do better, go further, and stay more consistent, not only with your spiritual lives but with your lives together in general, if you start early. And you don't have to do any of this on your own. There are literally thousands of resources out there: on the Internet, at your local Catholic bookstore, the mobile app that goes with this book, and at your parish. Talk to your priest and maybe he can even recommend a slightly older couple to mentor you, or talk to your folks, or your aunt who's family always seemed to get this better than yours did, or your grandpa, or someone else whom you trust. Whatever you do, just *do something*, do it right away, and just start. If nothing else, at least begin to pray the "Couple's Prayer;" or better, write one of your own you can say together each night before bed. As with everything else we've presented here, *make it your own*.

## Recap

## Why is prayer so important, especially in the life of a couple?

- Why do most couples report that praying together is so difficult?

- What are some good examples of the Church's liturgical or devotional life you can incorporate into your own family practice? Do either of your families of origin have traditional ethnic or religious practices which would help give you a starting point?
- How will you two pray as a couple tonight?

# CONCLUSION: *Ite, Missa Est*

These are the last words of the Mass and are notoriously difficult to translate. You're probably most familiar with, "The Mass is ended. Go in peace." Or something like that. *Ite* certainly means "Go!" The trouble is that the *missa est* part means "*It* is sent," not "*You* are sent." The members of the assembly are not "its," plus the assembly is otherwise always addressed in the you-plural form. What, then, is the *it* being sent? The most common opinion is that it is the Church as a whole; that we are not sent on a mission alone but altogether, and so at the end of every Mass it is the whole Church who is sent to proclaim the good news and glorify God by their lives. This must be preeminently true of married couples and families, not only because they make up the bulk of almost every assembly at Mass but also because their very experience of *mission* is always and precisely in common.

This book began by asking the question, "Why are you reading this book?" It offered some answers at the outset but hopefully by now you have a much richer understanding of why *you,* and hopefully better why *both of you,* have read it. Often books seem to come to us at just the right moment in our lives. Other times they come and we even intuit as we're reading that now is not the time, so either we shelve it and wait until later, or finish it and then return when it seems right. Whether you are married or getting married, totally on board with all the Church says or still seriously struggling with some teaching, a devout Catholic or getting married to one, this book should at least have given you a good sense of what's possible in a marriage. *The Mission of Love* laid out in this book isn't easy but is possible, and there are couples all around you managing it right now. But they haven't done it by themselves and they don't do it by themselves now either. They do it in the Church, with the Church, and for the Church, inasmuch as *they are the Church.* That's the *Mission* which has been given to you or will be given to you when you marry: to share the good news that Jesus is risen from the dead, *together.*

## The First Day of the Rest of Your Lives

The Christian life is ultimately one of *conversion*. Conversion means literally to "turn around." Ongoing, daily conversion is the work of the Christian life. It doesn't happen mostly in church, though that's certainly part of it, but it happens at the office, in your home, in the van on the way to soccer practice, and at your favorite restaurant on a date. That thing in your partner that makes you want to be better than you are right now, that's how your partner is helping to save you. That's how your partner administers the sacrament of matrimony to you. That's how your spouse keeps you faithful to your baptism.

The best thing about conversion is that it's never over. Even if you were a convert to the Faith as an adult, the work of conversion is never, ever done. Each new day is the first day of the rest of your life—your lives, *together*. That's why marriage is so important, and why your spouse is so important to you in particular. Romantic comedies and fairy tales want us to believe that fate or the universe or some other impersonal power has destined each one of us for another. Our claim is even bolder. God has formed this spouse for you—*for you*—so that you could be uniquely suited to help wear off one another's rough patches and improve one another's character. You were made for the greatest of things—heaven—and you were made to help each other get there.

## In the World, But Not of the World

How you arrive at the goal of your marriage is as unique as are the two of you. The debits and credits, vices and virtues, character flaws and serious commitments, all these make up the person you are; your spouse helps you to determine the kind of Christian you will become.

This is a noble vision but it is not shared by all. Many today, and for most of history, have considered marriage to be simply an arrangement of convenience, or a concession to cultural norms, or even simply "all about love," though it is not always altogether clear what they mean by such "love." For this reason Christian spouses are called in a

146

preeminent way to be "in the world but not of the world." By the very way you live your wedded life together, which should be different than your non-Christian neighbors, you give witness to God-in-the-flesh, to Jesus' life, death, and resurrection. You give hope of something more to come.

This "in the world but not of the world" dynamic is neither easy nor obvious. Holy Matrimony does make a couple into a "domestic church" even as baptism makes one a "little Christ," but that doesn't mean that you have to outfit your living room like a shrine any more than it means your husband has to grow out his beard and take up carpentry. The "in the world" bit means that you live in the world much as everyone else, much as Christians have from the very beginning. You work and you play, you take care of your family and fulfill your responsibilities, you pay your taxes and perform you civic duties, but you do not stop there. You also do more than take care of *your* family, you also befriend the poor and vulnerable. You do more than pay taxes: you make responsible decisions when you vote and you make clear to your candidates and officials which of their policies you find objectionable. You do work and play but you work and play *as a Christian*, as one who knows redemption and the forgiveness of her sins, and when you're able you make known the reason for the hope that is in you. But it happens in this way: quietly, subtly, and unpretentiously.

The "not of the world" clause is also important. This is what keeps us from muting our Christian witness or, worse, causing scandal because our lives are indistinguishable from anyone else's. You ought to live differently because of being a Catholic Christian. The sacraments, and first and foremost the sacrament of Holy Matrimony, should fuel and fulfill your life. Your belief in the Eucharist and the power of the Mass should make going to Church on Sunday something even more important for you than your non-Catholic friends. Your commitment to the truth and to virtuous behavior should form and determine your behavior differently than those who do not know the God who is Truth. This doesn't mean that Christians are smarter, better, or more virtuous than anyone else. What it does mean, however, is that we have more and better reasons for good marriages, loads more support and assistance, both internal and external, than we could ever actually use, and the promise of God to see us through and back us up all along the way.

## Romance vs. Intimacy

It's no accident that the word *romance* is so closely related to the word *Roman*. We Catholics, who have a special relationship to Rome, have as much reason to be *romantic* as anybody. And some of the best parts of our tradition make that clear: Arthur and Guinevere, Robin Hood and Marian, Dante and Beatrice, even John Kennedy and Jackie O. are ultimately the fruit of this tradition. Romance is a good and precious and holy thing when used rightly but it is not the *only* thing.

On its own, in the bastardized, dumbed-down, facile way that it gets presented today, romance is nothing more than fleeting emotion. But romance without commitment is simply trading reason for emotion. Romance without strength idolizes weakness. Romance without virtue is an excuse for vice. Romance without intimacy can never be truly called love.

Love, true love, the love we all long for and which most of us have long sought, the top-to-bottom, inside-to-outside, down in the belly to the marrow of my bones sort of love which moves mountains and spins stars, that sort of love requires intimacy. It's not to be found in one-night stands or friends-with-benefits arrangements; it's not the thoughtless sort of cohabiting that says, "let's see how it goes"; and it's most certainly not "I love you as you are and hope you never change." Love absolutely means having to say you're sorry, sometimes multiple times a day, but it also means saying, "I forgive you," as many times as it is honestly asked. Love means sometimes not liking your partner very much, or being very hurt by what they've done or how they've treated you. Love means seeing the gunk inside the other and loving them in spite of it, sometimes even because of it; not because of the gunk but because of how they've had to deal with it. What's more, love means letting the other see your gunk, seeing you not only at your best but at your worst. This is why romance on its own will always fail. Gallantry and chivalry can't hold a candle to honesty and integrity. When she sees that you don't always hold the door or put down the toilet seat, will she still love you? What's more, can she help form you into the sort of man who always does hold the door or put down the toilet seat, or at least tell the truth and do the right thing? Can you help her grow into the strong, independent, and creative sort of woman she longs to be? Can you support her in work and at home? Can you pitch in around the house to enable her to pursue her dreams, even as she does yours? Can you share with each other the deepest secrets in the quietest places of your heart – and live?

You remember John Mellencamp's story about "Jack and Diane"? Well, he was right, life does go on long after the thrill of living is gone. But the thrill of loving, truly loving, loving with the love which Christ Himself showed on the cross never stops, even if the tickles in your stomach ebb and flow. The most remarkable thing, though, is that even those bits of romance, even the thrill of living, lasts longer and are far more rewarding when rooted in intimacy.

## Freedom

"For freedom Christ has set us free," the Apostle reminds us, "so stand firm and do not subject yourself again to the yoke of slavery" (Galatians 5:1). What is this slavery? It's the cheap relationships and lackadaisical commitments which never really go anywhere. It's the giving of yourself on your own terms but always holding something back. It's inviting God into your relationship but only so far. It's committing to the Church but only as much as is comfortable. It's changing your life enough that you can feel it but not enough that you can't change it back. It's the false good that we give up when we commit ourselves to Christ in Christian marriage.

So what's the freedom? The freedom we inquire about before you exchange vows seems a good place to start:

> Have you come here *freely* and *without reservation* to give yourselves to each other in marriage?

Will you *love* and *honor* each other as man and wife for the rest of your lives?

Will you accept children lovingly from God, and bring them up according to the law of Christ and His Church?

Freedom, as St. Paul means it, and as you need it if you are to be successful in your marriage, is about radical openness. It's about giving of yourself *absolutely* to something *without reserve*. It's about committing yourself *finally* to one other person for rest of your life. And it's about accepting the gifts and the trials which God sends you. It's about keeping your word. These are serious commitments. It takes real freedom to make them. But you need that kind of freedom if your marriage is to be more than a polite arrangement for sharing property and occasionally having sex. If you want this relationship to be the dynamic, earth-shaking, world-changing reality that it promises to be, then you've got to have the interior and exterior freedom to give yourself to it as absolutely as you can right now, and as you continue to grow in freedom to give yourself to it more as life goes on. You should be able, at your twenty-fifth, and fiftieth, and seventieth anniversaries to look at your spouse and say honestly, "I love you more than I knew was possible that day so long ago."

That's true freedom. It may seem impossible, as it should, because by ourselves it is. With God, however, all things are possible.

> Promising love for ever is possible when we perceive a plan bigger than our own ideas and undertakings, a plan which sustains us and enables us to surrender our future entirely to the one we love. faith also helps us to grasp in all its depth and richness the begetting of children, as a sign of the love of the Creator who entrusts us with the mystery of a new person. (Pope Francis, *Lumen Fidei*, 52).

The gift of children signifies the other-orientation which the whole marital relationship is to take, and that's what permits us to give ourselves not only to one another in marriage but to complete strangers in Christian service.

## Couples for Others

Jesus was a "man for others." Christian couples, then, need themselves to be, both individually and collectively, "for others." The precise form this takes will vary, as everything, from couple-to-couple. This is why intimacy is so important. As you grow together you will discover the ways in which you two are best suited to give your lives for other people. Maybe that will be in terms of a year or two abroad as missionaries. Maybe it will be serving food at the soup kitchen once a week. Maybe it will be generously giving of your financial resources to the charities which need it most. Maybe it will be welcoming more children than is common into your family, or even accepting children by adoption, either from here or from some other country. Maybe it will just be about being dedicated members of your parish or devoted civil servants with a deep faith life. However you do it, your service to others and your witness to the world will ultimately be what determines whether or not you can accomplish your common mission.

This giving of one's self "for others" begins at home. You should be more generous with your spouse than with anyone else in the world. It's the reason you give your bodies to each other; not for convenience, nor to avoid an evil, but rather to do the greatest good which you can. Your life together: making breakfast, mowing the grass, taking care of her mother, putting up with his father, taking dance classes together, learning to garden, staying late for work, getting up early to jog, changing diapers, midnight feedings, teenage meltdowns, toddler tantrums, grown-up disappointments—you first learn to be "for the many" by being "for you" to your spouse.

The life of Christian spouses is to be deeply Eucharistic. This means, of course, regular reception of the Eucharist and hopefully frequent adoration too. But it also means, more profoundly, becoming what you eat and adore. It means saying with your lives what the priest says with his words: "This is my body...This is my blood...for you..." First, to your husband or wife, and then together to the Church and the world.

151

## Sacramental Signs

In this it becomes clear how marriage is and must be a sacrament. You are signs, and you are signs together which you could never be apart. You are signs of God's love, God's care, God's abiding presence with and for the human family. You communicate the grace of God to one another in your life together, and together you make that same graced life present to those who meet you. You are called, just as surely as those called to Orders or religious life are called, to make Christ known to the world.

And what's more, as ministers of God's redeeming love to the world, we actually get to participate in the very mystery which saves us. Just as a priest winds up being saved by the Paschal Mystery which he celebrates every time he offers Mass, so also the Christian couple are saved by the same mystery which they celebrate every time they catch dinner, make love, watch a sunrise, or mow the neighbor's lawn. In your spouse God has chosen to wrap you up in the greatest mystery of all, which is why in your spouse you will have a foretaste, a preview, a little taste of heaven. And hard as it is at times to believe, they will have the same of you.

## Beacons of Hope

When Pope Honorius III first confirmed the Dominican Order almost 800 years ago he called them "champions of the Faith and true lights of the world." The Dominicans have surely been that over the years but they don't have the market cornered. Each of us is called in virtue of our baptism to be the very same. You have been transformed, first by a mystery which you probably can't even remember, and now in a daily sort of way by a mystery which you can remember well but which is unfolding still right before your very eyes. Nothing will likely confound you or confuse you as much as your spouse and your relationship at times. Nothing will drive you crazier or give you more heartache but, if it works right, nothing will give you more joy, more peace, or more hope. Your spouse will be for you a sign of heaven, of the good things to come, and you will be the same for them.

But together you will be signs of the "something more" lurking just around the corner of everyday life. That "something more" we know by faith, and the Faith we come to know first and foremost in the family.

> Absorbed and deepened in the family, faith becomes a light capable of illumining all our relationships in society. As an experience of the mercy of God the Father, it sets us on the path of brotherhood. Modernity sought to build a universal brotherhood based on equality, yet we gradually came to realize that this brotherhood, lacking a reference to a common Father as its ultimate foundation, cannot endure. We need to return to the true basis of brotherhood.... As salvation history progresses, it becomes evident that God wants to make everyone share as brothers and sisters in that one blessing, which attains its fullness in Jesus, so that all may be one. The boundless love of our Father also comes to us, in Jesus, through our brothers and sisters. Faith teaches us to see that every man and woman represents a blessing for me, that the light of God's face shines on me through the faces of my brothers and sisters (Pope Francis, *Lumen Fidei,* 54).

Ultimately it is the Faith which makes true love possible. The kind of charity Christ has shown for His Church, which he bears to every creature in the universe, that kind of charity, that kind of love is just too big for us. Most of us are only able to manage it once in our lifetimes, and usually then with just one person, and even then only occasionally. But when we do manage it, when we do manage to get out of the way sufficiently to let God's grace do its work—well, it changes us, it makes us into more than we were, more than we thought we'd ever be, more than we dreamed we could be. It's the reason we get married and the reason we have children. And it's the reason that getting married makes all the difference in the world, not only to me and my spouse but to you and yours, and to people you don't even know and people you just haven't met yet. It's because the world needs, no actually *lives* on, this sort of love, whether everyone else realizes it now or not. And this kind of love, this kind of faith, makes you ready. It doesn't just prepare you, it actually gives you the ability to do something you never could have done before. It makes the two of you together infinitely better than you could ever have been apart, and it gives you the opportunity to change the world forever.

# AFTERWORD:
# Sign, Sex, and Sacrament

*"He said in reply, 'Have you not read that from the beginning the Creator 'made them male and female' and said, 'For this reason a man shall leave his father and mother and be joined to his wife, and the two shall become one flesh'? So therefore they are no longer two, but one flesh. Therefore, what God has joined together, no human being must separate."*

— *Mt 19:4-6*

*By it [the Sacrament of Matrimony] husband and wife are strengthened and ...consecrated for the faithful accomplishment of their proper duties, for the carrying out of their proper vocation even to perfection, and the Christian witness which is proper to them before the whole world."*

—*Paul VI, Humanae Vitae, 25.*

If you were to ask most people what makes the Catholic teaching on marriage distinctive they'd probably say something like, "Catholics don't believe in divorce," or "Catholics don't do birth control or gay marriage." This would all be correct but hardly unique to Catholics. More importantly, these only tell you what Catholics *don't* believe about marriage; they don't even *approach* what Catholics *do* believe about marriage and family life. If all you knew about baseball was that it wasn't football you might imagine a game more like soccer or hockey. In the same way an awful lot of people, both non-Catholics and Catholics, get an idea of what the Church's teaching on marriage is based on the "nots" that they know, rather than the "oughts" that the Church teaches. It's true that the Church teaches certain things have no place in the context of marriage in general or Christian marriage in particular but all of those "Thou shalt nots" are really conclusions—reasonable and true conclusions—that have been derived from the *positive* teaching on marriage and the family.

155

So if you had to use one word to talk about the distinctively Catholic view of marriage then what would it be? Hopefully "sacrament" or "sacramental." Broadly speaking, Catholics and Orthodox Christians believe that marriage is a sacrament, whereas Protestants do not. But this "Catholic difference" is important, even if one of you is a Protestant. Why? Because the "sacramentality" or sacramental quality of the relationship colors everything else that you do, which is why in this book we have worked so hard to help you protect, sustain, and direct your relationship to help you accomplish your *Mission of Love*.

## Chapter Objectives

- Explain what the Church means when it calls marriage a sacrament.
- Understand why freedom is so essential to the Catholic understanding of marriage.
- Explain the symbolic quality of sex in marriage.
- Understand why sex outside of marriage and sex within marriage, which is not open to life ultimately, says something different than what the Church believes.

## Saint-Making

The English word "sacrament" comes from the Latin *sacramentum* which means "to make holy" or "to consecrate." In the ancient world, the *sacramentum* was the ritual oath which a soldier took to Caesar in the Roman Empire. We might tend to think of military oaths as secular rather than sacred things but remember that Caesar was worshipped as a god, so that oaths sworn to him were something like vows made in a church. Because of that, the word *sacrament* carried with it both the sense of religiously consecrating something and the swearing of an oath—though this time to God and not to Caesar. In a certain way we can say that if the ancient Roman secular *sacramentum* made a man a soldier in Caesar's army then the Christian sacraments make Christians soldiers for Christ. Perhaps the better way to think of it is that the sacraments are the way that God "makes saints" in His Church.

The *Catechism of the Catholic Church* says that sacraments are "efficacious signs of grace, instituted by Christ and entrusted to the Church, by which divine life is dispensed to us" (1131). We tend to think of sacraments as particular moments which mark the passage of time or special events in a person's life. And indeed, some sacraments follow this pattern more than others and the meaning of the ritual itself often parallels the external situation of the person. Baptism celebrates new birth into Christ and is most frequently administered to those most recently born; Confirmation has important ties to Christian maturity and is often given in adolescence; Marriage and Holy Orders both mark commitments in the Church and in the world; and Anointing of the Sick is associated with sickness and death. But sometimes even those sacraments don't mark chronological age well: a person may be baptized on their deathbed, another might be confirmed as an infant, someone might be anointed because they are struggling with a serious illness but live for another fifty years, and someone else might be married or ordained when very ill or just before dying. More importantly, the two major sacraments which should make up the everyday life of most Christians—Confession and Holy Eucharist— don't really mark any particular period in the Christian's life; rather, they mark *every* period in the Christian life with their pattern of sin and forgiveness and the daily care which God gives His people. The point is that sacraments are not simply empty rituals or sociological ceremonies to mark the stages of life. They are what the Church says they are: *efficacious signs*—symbols that communicate what they represent—and gifts which bestow the divine life of grace. And not simply because the Church says so but because Christ Himself has given them.

Which comes to the dispute over the sacraments. At the time of the Reformation, the men we now call "the Reformers," (think of people like Martin Luther, John Calvin, Uldrich Zwingli) began to read the Scriptures in a way very different than many of their contemporaries. They each grew concerned in their own way that there was not sufficient evidence for all of the sacraments. Why? Because the Church had consistently claimed that Christ instituted the sacraments Himself, which is why her authority regarding them is limited (why, for instance, you can't baptize in hot cocoa or make Eucharist out of beer and pizza). But the Reformers, by and large, saw evidence only of baptism and Holy Eucharist in the scriptures (and confession, for Luther), and so Protestant communities down to this day generally speak of only two sacraments: Baptism and Holy Communion. Throughout the years different individuals and different groups have each proposed different configurations and schemas for the sacraments but the one which pretty much everyone has struggled with, even faithful Catholic theologians, is marriage. For we who are Catholics, then, or we who are to be married to Catholics and want to support them in their faith, we need to see why the Church insists that marriage is a sacrament and why that matters, not only here but hereafter.

## Unsolved Mysteries

Part of the confusion stems from a problem of language. The word that comes into the Latin as *sacramentum* is really a Greek word, *mysterion*. In the Eastern Churches the sacraments are still called the "Holy Mysteries" and we have a vestige of this even in the Mass today when the priest invites the people at the beginning of Mass to "acknowledge our sins, that we might more worthily celebrate the *sacred mysteries.*" The word *mystery* itself is something of a problem, coming from *mu* and *sterion*. *Mu* is where we get our word *mute* from; *sterion* is a place where a sacred action takes place. So *mysterion* is an action which moves one to silent awe. It is used only once in the whole of the New Testament, and its use concerns us directly:

> For this reason a man shall leave (his) father and (his) mother, and be joined to his wife, and the two shall become one flesh.

> This is a great mystery but I speak in reference to Christ and His Church (Eph 5:31-33).

The one and only use of the word which *becomes* "sacrament" in English is in reference to marriage, the one sacrament that the experts in sacraments have trouble fitting into their regular categories.

Now a couple of things are worth saying here. The first is that *mystery* here is not the same as a novel you pick up at the airport or a show you watch on primetime. The sacred mysteries are not to be solved. Rather, these mysteries are something like the mystery of the sunrise, which can be explained through simple physical processes but which inspires awe and meditation as much as a rational conclusion. The mystery at play in St. Paul's letter is obviously the mystery of human love in marriage. Have you ever tried to "solve" your relationship? How'd that go for you? These aren't things to be solved but rather to be sat with. Christ's relationship to the Church is seen as a marriage, which is why in the scriptures He is constantly called "the bridegroom." Christians eventually came to call the Church "Mother" on the same grounds, because the life-giving, lovemaking which Christ offers His Church comes to full fruition in the sacraments and literally *births* new Christians in baptism. So rather than struggle to put marriage in the philosophical categories of sacramental theology, the sacraments themselves need to be approached and explained in the way very much like one would try to explain his relationship to his wife.

Not only that, but in establishing himself as bridegroom of the Church, Christ "elevated marriage to the dignity of a sacrament." Now what does this mean? The Reformers thought that it meant that Christ had to have presided over at least one wedding celebration in his lifetime. The Wedding at Cana was the natural choice but of course Jesus didn't "preside" over that in any way that we would recognize today. It is of course significant that Christ's first miracle happened at a wedding but the couple at Cana were not the first to have a sacramental marriage, if for no other reason than that they were (presumably) not baptized! No, Christ did indeed institute the sacrament of marriage but not in quite the way He instituted the others. This one was special because it was from the beginning.

Unlike the other sacraments, which Christ established during his earthly ministry, marriage has been a sacrament of sorts from the very beginning. "Be fruitful and multiply," the Lord tells the first man and woman. "Fill the earth and subdue it." Gen 1:28, the rabbis call this the "first commandment" because it is the first real direction given by God to human beings. And it is important to notice that in the Genesis account the "marriage" of the man and woman precedes the fall; that is, marriage in origin is without sin. So don't let anyone try and tell you that Original Sin is about sex. It's just not true; sex preceded the Fall and didn't even become a problem until sin first entered the equation through disobedience. So while sex is certainly one of those areas most deeply affected by our sinful natures it is not identical with it. This is important because it means that there is a good, proper, and holy way to live out and express our sexuality apart from celibacy. It's what we do in Christian marriage, and God called it "very good."

## A Natural Sacrament?

Okay, well Jesus is God, and so as God we can say that he established marriage from the beginning of human history. But how could that possibly represent the love which He has for His Church? There are at least two ways of getting at this question, and they're both important for understanding the Catholic teaching on marriage and human sexuality. First of all, the *matter* of the sacraments, the *stuff* of them, all predate the sacraments themselves. This was intentional on God's part, as St. Peter himself shows us.

> For Christ also suffered for sins once, the righteous for the sake of the unrighteous, that he might lead you to God. Put to death in the flesh, he was brought to life in the spirit. In it he also went to preach to the spirits in prison, who had once been disobedient while God patiently waited in the days of Noah during the building of the ark, in which a few persons, eight in all, were saved through water. This prefigured baptism, which saves you now. It is not a removal of dirt from the body but an appeal to God for a clear conscience, through the resurrection of Jesus Christ, who has gone into heaven and is at the right hand of God, with angels, authorities, and powers subject to him (1 Pt 3:18-22).

Water doesn't just predate baptism, it predates the whole of human history, and wrapped up in baptism is the whole history of humankind's relationship to water. Because of this, baptism can be a sign both of death and the tomb, Christ's descent into Hell, God saving Noah and his family in the ark, the Exodus of Israel from Egypt through the Red Sea, and of the washing of the body. Because it is such a potent sign, baptism makes present a host of realities. It doesn't *just* forgive sins (though that would be enough) but also has the new Christian share in Christ's death and resurrection, saves them from the powers of sin and wickedness, sets them free for a new life of grace, and brings them up in a community of love. Marriage is very much the same. As a natural symbol human lovemaking symbolizes an act of paramount communion between two people, it establishes and renews that couple in a particular relationship within the Church and society, and if not interfered with it brings forth new life.

Secondly, the *form* of the sacrament, the *way in which it's celebrated* (words, gestures, actions, etc.) articulate the meaning of the matter in the sacramental context. Parents bathe their babies all of the time but they aren't re-baptizing them each time they wash them. "I baptize you in the name of the Father, and of the Son, and of the Holy Spirit," tells us what kind of washing this is. What, then, is the *form* of marriage? Well, part of the reason some people have struggled with marriage as a sacrament is because the whole matter gets a little bit fuzzy. Certainly the words are important, so let's look at them:

> I (name) take you (name) to be my wife (husband). I promise to be true to you in good times and in bad, in sickness and in health, to love you and honor you all the days of your life.

Of course, the vows can also come in the form of questions, as in "Do you, (name), take (name), to be your wife? The formula is the same for the bride and the groom, except of course for the words "husband" and "wife." Notice too that the words used are not "bride" and "groom" which refer only to the day of the wedding, these establish a relationship meant to last.

This is why the Church doesn't permit people to just make up their own vows. We've probably all seen that before, either in real life or in various media, but the thing is that the Church means something very specific by what she intends a couple to accomplish in marriage. A person could try to make up their own vows and they might get more or less what the Church means but they might not. More importantly, by reciting the same vows everyone else does when they get married in the Church, the couple is reminded that their relationship exists within the context of a much wider network of relationships which extend out far beyond simply friends and family to the whole of the Church, living and deceased.

Remember how the word *sacrament* was related to oath-taking? Well it still is, and those oaths are so important that before the Church lets people make them they have to first show that they know what they're doing, that they're free to do so, and what the consequences of their actions are. Freedom and responsibility are the name of the game. In fact, this is why Karol Wotyla, later to become John Paul II, names his important work *Love and Responsibility*. He knew that there were a lot of false ideas about freedom running around but that true freedom was really found in giving yourself away.

This question of freedom is really at the heart of the Catholic notion of marriage. Most of us default to an idea of freedom which more or less boils down to "I can do whatever I want, whenever I want to," with the possible caveat, "So long as it is neither hurting nor bothering other people." This is really a horrible idea of freedom because then most of the arguments we wind up having about whether or not a law is just is whether or not limiting a particular freedom actually hurts or bothers anybody. What's worse, anybody who has ever known anyone with an addiction knows that "wanting" is a whole lot more complicated than it really looks. A junkie really *wants* his fix but that doesn't mean that he should have it, and it *definitely* doesn't mean he's free.

The kind of freedom we're talking about here is the natural freedom of the human person—the kind we were made with from the beginning. It does involve being free of external constraints but the constraints in question here would have to do mostly with whether or not the person was already married (you can't give yourself to another if you've already given yourself away to someone else); or if you are already committed in some other way (a priest or religious has already given themselves away in a totally different fashion and would mean that they're not free to do so in marriage). It also means that you have the capacity to do what you say you're going to; this is why children can't get married, since they don't yet have the faculties, physically, mentally, or morally, to fulfill what it is they'd be promising. Likewise, people that can't have sexual intercourse can't be married. Why? Because they wouldn't be able to fulfill their vows. This doesn't mean that couples that know they are infertile can't marry. First of all, the Bible is full of seemingly infertile couples who seem to have babies by a special act of God. But more importantly, that's because the couples in question theoretically *could* have children, inasmuch as the nature of a man and a woman are designed to have children, but some internal pathology got in the way. It seems pretty hard to claim that the Church is anti-sex, though, when it demands that people be able to have it in order to be married, and in normal circumstances at least presumes that it will be a regular, integral, and spiritually essential part of their life together.

## Speaking with Our Bodies

The lovemaking of husband and wife is a symbolic act. It speaks with the body what the mouth said at the wedding. "I promise to be true to you...I will love you and honor you...as long as we both shall live." Words of love find their fulfillment in the act of love. The gift of self is shown in the gift of one's body. John Paul II wrote about this at length in what we now call the "Theology of the Body." The basic principle is this: we have bodies. God gave them to us on purpose. But we're more than just bodies, we're intellects and wills, minds and hearts too. And these all work together to form a whole. And that whole needs to act together for our acts to be truly human. So the most human of acts are those that use at once the body, mind, and heart. In the natural order of things, there's nothing else that does this like lovemaking in marriage. And because in the natural order that God set up this is the highest, best, and most symbolic of actions, so in the supernatural order which God established in the Incarnation it remains both the highest human expression of love as well as a sign of something more. That something more is ultimately revealed in Jesus.

Jesus showed us what that "something more" was at the Last Supper. "Take and eat, this is my body...Drink from it, all of you, for this is my blood of the covenant, which will be poured out for you and for many..." He gave Himself, body and soul for us. So too we are to give ourselves, body and soul, to and for each other. And just as when the Church celebrates the Eucharist she always does so "in memory of Him," and this remembering makes Him present again, so also whenever a Christian couple make love, mindful of their love and wanting to renew their commitment to one another, they not only rededicate themselves to each other but they also give glory to God and make Jesus present in a very particular and unique sort of way.

This is why the Church takes sex so seriously. Most people are inclined to think that the Church hates sex, or thinks sex is always bad, or that bodies are bad, or that every sexual thought, word, or deed is a sin. It's not true; it's just that every sexual thought, word, or deed, is potentially sacramental, and so to take it out of its proper context is not only to lose control of an appetite but to commit a kind of sacrilege. Sex before marriage, what the Church calls fornication, is a sin not because its sexual but because its sex out of context. Adultery, that is, sex when one or another partner is already married, is a sin not because it's sex but because it's sex with the wrong person and in somebody else's context. Ultimately these are wrong because they are a lie; you can't reseal a covenant you haven't made yet, and you can't rededicate yourselves to promises you haven't given yet. Now it's certainly true, you can tell greater and lesser lies on this score but the seriousness of a lie depends not only on *what* you say but also *to whom* you tell it. Sex with your fiancée might seem like it's not such a big deal, since sooner or later you'll be having sex anyway. But telling yourselves this lie about each other now only promises confusion once you're actually married. Obviously casual sex, either random hook-ups or acquaintance sex or whatever tells a bigger lie; you're actually not interested in giving yourself to this person and you may even say that with your mouth but with your body you say, "I'm yours." But these lies, though they are worse deceptions, are by definition to people who care for you less. That's why the Church tells us to do neither: don't sin against your sexuality and against your spouse, whether present or future, by telling lies with your body about yourselves and each other.

## Learning the Language of Communion

Loving communion in the marital sense has its own language. It's not something you learn in a day or a week or a month or even a year. It doesn't begin on your wedding day or in your bed on your wedding night, though if all is working to the good you would be speaking it both places. You should have spoken your first words this way early on in your relationship, and you should continue to grow in your "vocabulary" and "grammar" as you move along. This consists of the whole host of interactions which you have with one another: long conversations and short texts, learning to read one another's emotions and personalities, small acts of kindness and devotion, and signs of affection and love. As with any interaction, whatever you "say" winds up "speaking" not only *to* your Beloved but also *about* you.

This tends to be the place where most other sexual sins happen. Masturbation, using pornography, oral, anal, or other sex which doesn't ultimately wind up in vaginal intercourse, these are all serious defects in your personal grammar and vocabulary. Obviously they are often formed by years of "speaking" wrongly before you ever met your partner and, as with any other character flaw or moral struggle, a patient partner will at once both challenge and affirm you as you develop better habits. The point here is that all of these things take what is literally intended to be among the highest of realities and make them something less—sometimes something much less.

That being said, much as someone who has had a stroke may need some help learning to speak again, sometimes there will be a deficit or an injury so significant that you can't work it out together. Past relationships, previous marriages, a history of physical, emotional, or sexual abuse, and other psychological and emotional problems can be real barriers to authentic and integral intimacy. Sometimes these things need to be addressed, at least to some degree, before a marriage can even take place. A person with a history of sexual abuse who has never been to counseling may, for instance, not really be capable of an authentic sexual relationship; likewise, a person with serious trust issues form childhood may not be able to experience genuine intimacy. Many times, however, issues only come to the surface after the marriage has taken place. This is a time when it is most incumbent upon the spouse to be supportive and help their partner to get help. There are a host of resources available pretty much wherever you are but your local Catholic Charities is often a good place to start. They can refer you to good Catholic counselors or may even be able to provide some of their own. Most importantly, they'll help you find people who can help you work through these issues and so enter more deeply into a vital and loving relationship.

In the natural order, the way things are in the world just by being what they are, a married couple stands as a kind of natural symbol of the Trinity. God the Father gives Himself eternally and perfectly to the Son; God the Son eternally receives the gift of the Father and gives Himself in return; this mutual act of giving and receiving love is so perfect and profound that it constitutes a third Person—the Holy Spirit. Likewise, a man loves a woman and gives himself totally, perfectly, and exclusively to her. She receives his act of love and reciprocates in kind. Their mutual love constitutes a kind of "third person" in the relationship itself. This is manifest most perfectly when the "third person" actually takes on concrete form in another living person—that is, when lovemaking results in the conception of a child.

## Inconceivable!

By the number of jokes about it in the media you'd think that everyone in the world knows that the Catholic Church is opposed to birth control. And yet priests who regularly preach on it consistently get responses from people suggesting that they've never heard of the teaching. This is especially strange historically since every other Christian denomination was opposed to artificial contraception until the 1920s. In any case, to remove all ambiguity,

> Therefore We base Our words on the first principles of a
> human and Christian doctrine of marriage when We are obliged

once more to declare that the direct interruption of the generative process already begun and, above all, all direct abortion, even for therapeutic reasons, are to be absolutely excluded as lawful means of regulating the number of children. Equally to be condemned, as the magisterium of the Church has affirmed on many occasions, is direct sterilization, whether of the man or of the woman, whether permanent or temporary. Similarly excluded is any action which either before, at the moment of, or after sexual intercourse, is specifically intended to prevent procreation—whether as an end or as a means. (*HV* 14)

These words come from Pope Paul VI in his encyclical (an important kind of papal document) *Humanae Vitae*. They're pretty clear. Abortion is wrong because it ends the life of a child. Direct sterilization is wrong because it permanently removes the possibility of procreation from the act of lovemaking. And artificial birth control is wrong because it removes the possibility of procreation from the act of lovemaking, at least in particular instances or for periods of time.

This is a hard teaching and many do not accept it. Of course, Jesus had other hard teachings too (see John 6:68). All of the ins and outs of the Church's teaching on artificial contraception are beyond the scope of this book. Your diocese should have a Family Life Office which can get you more information on this, and there should be classes on Natural Family Planning in your area. Inasmuch as it touches on marriage as a sacrament, however, it is at least worth looking at artificial contraception from the perspective of the sign value of married love.

When married Christians give themselves to one another in sacred lovemaking, they renew, reseal, and re-present the covenant they made on the day of their wedding. Instead of an animal being split in two they were themselves split in two: the woman as she received the man into her body, and the man as his seed separated from him as a gift to his wife. It's certainly true that not each and every act of sexual intercourse results in the birth of a child: the Church doesn't think so and it doesn't expect so, but it does expect that in the total gift of self which spouses are asked to give to each other that this includes one's ability to procreate. Otherwise what you're saying is essentially, "You can have all of me but this part." That's not a marriage. It might be a committed relationship. There might be real love there. But it's not the total gift of self to the other for the sake of the other and the whole world that Christian marriage is.

Condoms and IUDs are actually a kind of anti-sacrament. They stand as physical barriers to the natural sign which is meant to signify love. They make clear what's going on in the act: "I'm holding back, I'm giving you part of me but not all of me." Chemical contraception in all of its forms is more insidious because you can't see it. A pill which you take daily or otherwise seems to be unrelated to the gift of self which happens sometime later but given that the pill is being taken *for the sake of making one's self incapable of giving all of herself*, it acts just like a condom or an IUD. People think that the Church's concern is with the artificial nature of contraception. That's part of it, to be sure: contraception treats conception and pregnancy like a disease, but the real issue is intent. The Church is calling the card on the intent of the couple trying on purpose not to conceive. Because she thinks every act of lovemaking should result in a baby? No. Because she thinks every act of lovemaking ought to be an authentic gift of self, and if you've temporarily sterilized yourself to prevent pregnancy then you're not giving all of yourself, only a chemically-altered, now-slightly-less version of yourself. But that's not what Christian love is for, and eventually that shows itself in the marriage.

Likewise Natural Family Planning is not simply "Catholic Birth Control." Natural Family Planning (NFP) is about *planning*, and it plans both the conception and spacing of children as well as the individual acts of love around the natural cycles of the woman. With the use of NFP, it is not the birth of a child that is being controlled but, rather, the will and desires of individuals towards a prayerfully discerned goal. It has gotten a terrible reputation in certain gynecological circles and unfairly so. When used properly it is far more effective than condoms and comparable to most chemical contraceptives. But of course, the effectiveness of NFP cannot be measures simply in births that it prevents—it must also be measured by the births that it produces, because Natural Family Planning presumes that one is actually planning on having a family. The symbolism here is obvious. The husband and wife become keenly aware of the wife's cycle and the internal motions of her body. Together they grow in an intimacy they never could have dreamed of before. And their knowledge of one another and the intimacy which they have breathes forth, ultimately, in a new person.

The point here is simply this: Artificial contraception, of whatever sort, militates absolutely against the symbolic and sacramental reality which Christians call marriage. Natural Family Planning, rightly used, actually enhances it. The Church's continued opposition to contraception is ultimately because as couples grow in love, to hold back that significant a part of you should be literally *inconceivable!*

## Signs of Things to Come

The Church's teaching on sex and marriage—especially in this day and age—is hard to accept and hard to live up to. Nobody does it perfectly, nobody ever has, but frustrations in the moral life should never cause us to give up. Most of us persist in telling at least white lies for most of our life, and yet few of us find ourselves so crippled by a guilty conscience that we can't get up and go to work in the morning for fear of telling a fib; less still do we create complicated theories to explain why lying is not only acceptable in certain circumstances but probably to be preferred. The problem is that even the institution of marriage has been touched by sin, and because necessarily every marriage is composed of two sinful people they both have a tendency to think that the marriage is about them alone.

To this the Church points to the natural dimensions of marriage. Marriage has always been about three things: the couple, the kids, and everybody else. Marriage, even in the natural order, is about the couple inasmuch as it is ordered to stabilizing loving relationships and regulating sexual relationships. The state has a vested interest in regulating sex for both health and reproductive reasons, and it regulates romantic couplings to ensure good order and the care of children. Marriage is about kids inasmuch as children have a natural right to both their mother and their father as the source of their life and that the ordinary way in which a child is to experience both is in the context of a marriage. This is, incidentally, part of the reason that states have historically regulated marriage: being married presumed that the woman's husband was the legal father of her children (even though in point of fact he might not be). Finally, marriage is about "everybody else" in terms of the society, whether that was a small clan or a large empire. In stabilizing relationships, marriage stabilizes society, makes clear where people stand, and ensures that children are born into situations in which they can be cared for.

And yet *Christian Marriage*, or the Sacrament of Holy Matrimony, is a different thing still. It is entirely possible that a couple can be a sign of the Trinity on the natural level and have no knowledge of it. It is not possible for Christians to be a sign of Christ's love for His Church without knowing and intending it.

> The sacrament of Matrimony signifies the union of Christ and the Church. It gives spouses the grace to love each other with the love with which Christ has loved his Church; the grace of the sacrament thus perfects the human love of the spouses, strengthens their indissoluble unity, and sanctifies them on the way to eternal life. (*Catholic Church* 1661)

The danger in calling marriage a "natural sacrament" is that it might suggest that all marriages are fundamentally the same, which they are not. Marriage is a natural good in and of itself, and predates Judaism, Christianity, and human society itself. Because God has ordered it in the way that He has, it functions as a kind of efficacious symbol—a sign which accomplishes what it represents—namely the union and betterment of the couple and through them of the society.

When we say that Jesus "raised" or "elevated" marriage to the dignity of a sacrament, however, we mean something altogether different. Baptized Christians by their very nature, which has been transformed by faith and baptism, are already "little Christs" and called to proclaim the kingdom of God. Marriage among Christians is a sacrament because in the Christian life Christ has taken the natural institution of marriage which already stood for something more than it was all by itself and has given it eternal significance. Christian marriage is now an eschatological sign—a sign of the things to come—inasmuch as Christian spouses make present and incarnate the love which Christ has for His Church. If the Church's moral teaching on marriage and sexuality seems like a pretty tall order that's because it is—and ought to be:

> The gift of the sacrament is at the same time a vocation and commandment for the Christian spouses, that they may remain faithful to each other forever, beyond every trial and difficulty, in generous obedience to the holy will of the Lord: "What therefore God has joined together, let not man put asunder." (John Paul II, *Familiaris Consortio*, 20)

# APPENDIX:
# Cohabitation and other Considerations

There is an understandable appeal to cohabitation when the odds of being hurt by a failed relationship are so high. If you're going to commit the whole of your life to another person, it would only seem logical that you would want to know as much about that other person beforehand. With cohabitation you have, or at least potentially have, all of the perceived benefits of marriage: shared space, goods, resources, proximity to one another, opportunity for regular sex (if that's part of the arrangement—it isn't always), and the chance to get to know your partner really, really well. At the same time it lacks the commitment of marriage, and so if you break up, it's not quite like getting divorced.

But that's part of the problem: it is a lot more like getting divorced than breaking up with your boyfriend who lives across town. Leases have to be broken, property divided up, you have to get used to living alone again—everything changes. Which is part (though certainly not the only) reason that the Church remains opposed to cohabitation—it limits your freedom. A person is just less likely to call the whole thing off the more entangled they've become.

Now that's not to say that all cohabitating couples are the same or that they choose to do it for the same reasons. And no one should presume that because a couple is cohabitating before marriage that they're having sex. That's important, because the Church still discourages cohabitation even if the couple pledges to remain chaste. Why? Because living together is a public act: you make contracts, sign leases, share major purchases, and these all suggest one thing: you're married, when, in fact, you are not. This makes it all the more difficult to understand what happens when you finally do get married. This is hands-down the most common question that couples who have been cohabiting for some time bring to marriage prep: What difference will the marriage make?

Many couples wind up living together out of convenience. She's sleeping over at his place so often, or he's so seldom actually in his apartment, that it simply stops making sense to keep separate spaces. But do you really want your marriage to be based on convenience? Did you first ask her out because it was easy? Did you fall in love with him because it was convenient? Or did you feel drawn to one another, have you grown because of the other, are you better because of each other? And if so, doesn't that demand something different?

So, there are three points to be made up front: cohabitating before marriage does not necessarily spell doom for your relationship, not all cohabitating couples are the same, and the strategies and activities in this book should work equally well for those couples who have been cohabitating and for those who have not. Statistically speaking, what is important about cohabitation is what Dr. Scott Stanley has called a "sliding" vs. a "deciding" mentality. Couples that get engaged or are at least clear on getting married before they cohabitate have a much better chance than those who just slide into it. Spiritually speaking, this is significant too. After all, who wants to blunder into love or stumble into marriage uncommitted, undecided, and unprepared?

The "together forever" promise of marriage is something more than just living together. It's about committing to each other permanently, absolutely, so that together you'll be free to pursue your life's work together. That's not something that can be practiced on a trial basis but is an all-or-nothing commitment. And that work is more than just your own; in fact, it's something that we all share in as part of the Church. It's also the reason the Church cares about your relationship to start with.

Cohabitation, then, puts both the couple seeking to get married in the Church and the priests, deacons, lay ministers, and sponsor couples assigned to work with them in a very awkward and difficult situation. Though it is not often taught explicitly that cohabitation is a serious problem, most couples intuit that there's something wrong, or at the very least, that the people at church won't like it very much. Sometimes they'll just lie about it but this is always a mistake: first, because you shouldn't be lying at all, let alone to the Church, and especially when you're asking them to help you get married; second, because at this point in time a couple coming to get married who aren't cohabitating is so rare that it actually draws more attention to their living situation and not less. Some couples will be pretty straight about it, explain how they arrived at the decision to cohabitate, and then discuss what they've learned from the situation; but most will mention it briefly and then try and bluster through it to something else. And the worst part is, priests, deacons, and sponsor couples often let them get away with it.

Virtually everyone in the Church who works with couples, and plenty of non-Catholic and even secular counselors also, know the kind of damage that cohabitation can do to a relationship. At the same time, nobody seems to know what to do about it. Many won't even ask the question, "Are you living together?" for fear of getting the wrong answer. Others will ask, offer a "tsk, tsk" or a disapproving look, and then move on to other less anxiety-producing questions. Still others recognize that cohabitation is wrong, have a sense of why they think that is, but whose only solution is to get the couple to separate for a while. Sometimes this comes in the form of an ultimatum, "The diocese (or parish) has a policy that says we can't marry you if you don't separate for six months before the wedding," or something like that. Other times the conversation more closely resembles haggling in a market, "Can you try moving out for just three months? How 'bout two months? What if you just separated for a couple of weeks?" The suggestion that a time of separation can be useful is not a bad one but the problem is that simply separating for a few weeks, or even a couple months, doesn't really hit the reset button on the relationship. It might help the pair to avoid sexual sin in the weeks just before the wedding (though those who want to get past that always will) but it fails to address the real problem of cohabitation and the dangers which it poses for a marriage.

The problem with cohabitation is not simply sex, though sex before marriage is both sinful and psychologically, emotionally, and personally problematic. Neither is it just about scandal (the idea that a practicing Catholic would be living in a public way which is opposed to the Church's teaching), though that's a big deal too. No, the problem with cohabitation before marriage is essentially the problem with sex before marriage. Sex not only *does* something between the couple, it *says something too*—both to the couple, and to the rest of us. Sex in marriage is a sign of something else, something big, and something which sex outside of marriage can never totally signify. Cohabitation, literally setting up your public self and living situation as though you were married when in fact you are not, likewise says something—something which is not altogether true—at least not yet. Living in that tension, between what your public self is saying and what your private self knows to be the case, makes the boundaries of your relationship extremely unclear. Fuzzy boundaries lead to mismatched expectations, and mismatched expectations lead to serious conflict and disappointment, and all of these outside of the context of a clearly and publicly committed relationship work against the success of that relationship and often lead to its failure.

But the answer cannot simply be to slide a pamphlet with a bunch of statistics across a desk to a couple which tells them that their relationship is already doomed. Nor can it be simply to have the couple separate for a few months and pretend that the relationship will magically heal itself or return to the place it was before. Cohabitation sets up patterns of relationship, patterns which are normally dependent upon the commitment which comes from marriage but without the benefit of the commitment itself. So part of the Church's pastoral care to cohabiting couples *must* be helping couples work through these patterns of relationship and helping them to see just what kind of a difference marriage really makes.

Make no mistake, the authors of this book are not suggesting that cohabitation is okay. We stand with the Church and support her teaching; at the same time, we recognize that the pastoral care of cohabiting couples is one of the most pressing issues in the Church today and that many of the practices currently floating around are not only ineffective but also sometimes alienating, damaging, and counterproductive.

The ultimate decision about "what to do" with any particular couple always rests with the local pastor, as it should. He's the one who, with the direction of his bishop, needs to assess each situation and decide whether a separation is necessary and what sort of premarital counseling or preparation needs to be completed before the marriage can take place. Not all cohabiting couples are the same and different situations call for different responses. A couple who has been "just trying it out" for six months or a year is in a very different sort of a position than an engaged couple sharing a space they mean to make their own for the last two or three months of an engagement. And these are different still from the immigrant couple with two or three kids who have been afraid to marry for fear of being reported to the government. The Church entrusts the care of these couples to their parish priests on purpose, because they should know them, and they should be able to reasonably and prudentially decide what is best in conjunction with the couples themselves.

But no one today should be making such decisions alone. And no one should be trying to enter into a marriage in the Church, especially if they have been cohabiting, without first at least examining the patterns of relationship that make up their common lives together. This book has been written with a special eye towards cohabiting couples and their particular needs, though the strategies and activities provided and the reflections included certainly would apply to all couples to greater and lesser degrees. This book is also meant to help the minister assigned to work with couples to develop some criteria and direction in making decisions about premarital preparation, practice, and counseling.

## Mixed Marriages

Every book makes assumptions about its readers. We've done our best to minimize that here but even we couldn't avoid it. So the main assumption of the book is that it is being read by one or both parties in a couple that is married, engaged, or at least thinking about what marriage might mean to them. We have made this assumption mindful of the fact that others will use the book, especially priests and deacons involved in marriage prep, but when the book speaks in the second person to "You," our intended audience, it presumes a couple. We assume that the rest of you can figure that out.

In a similar way, this book makes presumptions about the type of couples who will be using it. As we noted above, the book recognizes that many, if not most, of the couples reading it will already be living together, and it tries to take that into account as it reflects on the meaning of marriage and the activities it presents. The book also presumes that the marriages it will be assisting are sacramental. This means that both of the parties are baptized Christians and, ideally, are both Catholic. Of course this is often not the case, and we certainly don't want to give short shrift to couples entering into mixed marriages, but it simply isn't possible to address every potential situation in the course of a book. We've tried to address this some with the examples throughout the book but a few words here might help to set the stage for couples coming into this from different faith traditions.

The vision and theology of marriage presented in this book is unapologetically Catholic. It is rooted deeply in the liturgical and magisterial tradition of the Catholic Church. Part of what makes the Catholic tradition *Catholic* is that it is distinct from other traditions. Orthodox Christians should identify pretty closely with much of what's written here but for many Protestants the Catholic theology of marriage can really seem like a foreign language. It's a really important language to learn, however, if you plan on being married to a Catholic, because even if they haven't been a super-practicing Catholic for a while, this is the implicit, subconscious vision of marriage which they've got. This means that you need to at least understand it and sign on to as much of it as you can, so that you can be clear about what you all disagree on. Disagreement need never spell the end of a relationship, even disagreement about the most important things, but it's important to be clear about what it is you disagree and agree on.

This is even truer for marriages between Catholics and non-Christians. That isn't to say that any of these marriages are impossible but the Church makes a clear distinction between marriages between Christians and marriages among Christians and non-Christians. It's not because we believe in second-class marriages but because Christian marriage is a sign of Christ, and it would be profoundly disrespectful of the other person's belief, not to mention dishonest about the situation, to make the marriage of a Christian and a non-Christian a symbol of something the non-Christian doesn't even believe in. For that reason this book can be especially helpful for the mixed-religion couple. Even if your marriage lacks some of the elements which the book presumes, it should offer helpful insight into what the Church teaches about marriage and some of your spouse's presumptions—presumptions about which they may not even be aware themselves.

Marriages between Catholics and non-Catholics, especially when those non-Catholics are also non-Christians, do present a very particular set of issues. Clearly we can't address all of those here but we would recommend focusing in a very particular way on the chapters and activities which work on communication skills, conflict resolution, and expectations. The Vision Statement and overall purpose of these couples is going to be quite distinctive and that's okay, so long as everyone is clear about it moving forward and knows both the standard to which they will be held and the standard to which it is reasonable to hold their spouse. So if you fall into this category this book is for you, albeit in a very different way.

# ABOUT THE AUTHORS

## Dr. John Curtis, Ph.D.

Dr. Curtis has a bachelor's degree in Education, a Master's degree in Counseling and a Ph.D. in Human Resource Development. John currently provides organizational development services to public, private, and nonprofit organizations nationwide. Prior to serving as a business consultant, John was a full-time marriage counselor with clinical membership in the American Association for Marriage and Family Therapy. John and his wife have served as marriage facilitators and as a sponsor couple for marriage preparation in their parish. John has also provided marriage education nationwide for over thirty years. He is married with two children and three grandchildren.

## Fr. Dominic McManus, O.P.

Fr. McManus is a Dominican Friar of the Province of St. Albert the Great. He is adjunct instructor of liturgical and sacramental theology at the Aquinas Institute of Theology in St. Louis, Missouri.

## Mike Day

Mike Day has a bachelor's degree in Philosophy and is the Director of Marriage and Family Life for the Catholic Diocese of St. Augustine. He is married with two children and has worked in marriage ministry for over ten years.

# INDEX OF CITATIONS

Made in the USA
San Bernardino, CA
06 February 2014